The
Autobiography
of
Florence Kelley

The Autobiography of Florence Kelley

NOTES OF SIXTY YEARS

FIRST PERSON SERIES

Number One

FLORENCE KELLEY

NOTES OF SIXTY YEARS:

The Autobiography of Florence Kelley

With an Early Essay by the Author on
The Need of Theoretical Preparation
for Philanthropic Work

Edited & Introduced by
Kathryn Kish Sklar

Published for the Illinois Labor History Society by the

Charles H. Kerr Publishing Company

Chicago

1986

The Illinois Labor History Society
28 East Jackson
Chicago, Illinois 60604

This book has been funded in part by the
RALPH HELSTEIN FUND
FOR EDUCATION IN LABOR HISTORY

The photographs on the cover and frontispiece, and on pages 20, 21,
58, 59 and 75 are reproduced through the courtesy of the the Library
of the University of Illinois at Chicago (Jane Addams Memorial Col-
lection); those on pages 22, 44, 60, 76 and 90 through the courtesy
of the Manuscripts & Archives Division of the New York Public Library
(Nicholas Kelley Papers).

The publisher gratefully acknowledges the assistance of Claire Cass
of the Library of the University of Illinois at Chicago in locating many
of the photographs used in this book.

Cloth ISBN O-88286-092-5
Paperback 0-88286-093-3

Charles H. Kerr Publishing Company
Established 1886
P.O. Box 914
Chicago, Illinois 60690

Introduction

Without the spur of right-wing attacks on her as a "chief conspirator for Moscow," Florence Kelley might never have taken time from her reform work to write this brief but pointed autobiography. Originally published in 1926-27 as four articles in *Survey* magazine, Kelley's *Notes of Sixty Years* was "a call to action" against the rising tide of political reaction that threatened to destroy her lifetime of work on behalf of protective labor and social legislation for women and children.[1]

More than any other reformer in the Progressive Era (1880-1920), Florence Kelley led the struggle for the passage of labor and social legislation, including eight- and ten-hour day and minimum-wage legislation for women. Her historical importance was emphasized in 1953 by U.S. Supreme Court Justice Felix Frankfurter, who wrote that Kelley "had probably the largest single share in shaping the social history of the United States during the first thirty years of this century.... During that period hers was no doubt a powerful if not decisive role in securing legislation for the removal of the most glaring abuses of our hectic industrialization following the Civil War."[2]

Kelley focused her reform efforts on the passage of legislation
for women and children, but she and her contemporaries believed
that the effects of her campaigns extended beyond age-specific or
gender-specific populations to embrace all workers. The class-
specific meaning of her work was evident to Frankfurter and others
in the 1920s, including those who attacked her from the far right.

Kelley's memoirs were precipitated by the "red scare" of the
1920s when native-born American socialists like Eugene V. Debs
and Kate Richards O'Hare were imprisoned, and foreign-born
socialists were frequenty deported without a hearing. Since Kelley
was institutionally more closely affiliated with the social settlement
movement than with the Socialist Party, the political repressions of
that era affected her less directly than others, but in the mid- and
late 1920's she and Jane Addams became the targets of multiple
and concerted attacks by political extremists, first through
periodicals such as *The Woman Patriot*, and then by more
orthodox political groups, such as the Daughters of the American
Revolution.[3]

These attacks focused on Addams' pacifism and her unrelenting
opposition to American participation in World War I, but in
Kelley's case they emphasized her connections with international
socialism and Friedrich Engels. While Addams tended to ignore
this campaign to discredit her, Kelley tended to fight back. On one
occasion she proposed to Addams that they sue the DAR for libel,
thinking that it was one thing to be attacked scurrilously by
extremists like *The Woman Patriot,* another to be unfairly assaulted
by reputable national organizations. However, Addams did not
think they should take their case to court, and Kelley dropped the
proposal.

Writing these memoirs instead of going to court, Kelley saw them
as her way of demonstrating the legitimacy of her lifelong reform
efforts. In her sixty-seventh year she faced one of the most difficult
challenges of her career—how to save herself from the charge that
she was a political radical, when in many ways the charge was true,
since her social thought was shaped by the "scientific-materialistic
criticism" of Marx and Engels, and since she sought basic changes
in the relationship between the state and working women and
children.

In writing about her socialist commitments, Kelley had two
choices. She could provide a complete account and justify herself

as a socialist, or she could mask this dimension of her identity and emphasize other aspects of her life. Given the political environment of 1926, it is not too surprising that she chose the latter course. Therefore her reminiscences minimized her life-long participation in a variety of socialist organizations. Written for foe and friend alike, her *Notes of Sixty Years* was astutely political, and perhaps for that reason, did not always tell the whole story.

The late twentieth-century reader should be aware, therefore, that Kelley's presentation of herself in her *Notes* deserves to be augmented to include her commitment to socialist theory and practice. This edition seeks to do that in a brief introduction and by adding an example of Kelley's early writings, "The Need of Theoretical Preparation for Philanthropic Work."

Kelley devoted the third of her four autobiographical articles to the question of her socialist beliefs. "My Novitiate" dramatically described her youthful conversion to socialism in Zurich, Switzerland, when she was a graduate student there in 1883. In her conclusion, however, Kelley assured her readers that her "later thinking" was shaped more by her father and her early education than by the European socialism of her young adulthood. She concluded:

> My eager plunge into the enthusiasm of the new movement that was beginning to kindle throughout all Europe did not blind me to certain fundamental differences. Mine was after all an American background; those youthful years of talk with Father had whetted whatever discernment Nature had given me and those differences were to determine my later thinking.

This carefully worded disavowal of socialist influences in her "later thinking" emphasized the critical differences between the traditions of European socialism and her father's political traditions; she asserted that those differences "determined" her thinking. However, the statement leaves unmentioned a wide field of potential agreements between these two traditions, which tended to reinforce each other in Kelley's life work. It requires a careful reading to see that hers was not a general disavowal of socialist beliefs, but an acknowledgement that, when differences forced her to choose between the American and European traditions of reform, the native traditions won.

Kelley's friends knew that she considered herself a socialist most of her life, but many of her reform associates in the Consumers' League may not have realized it, for Kelley functioned as an independent political force. However important it might have been for her to think of herself as a socialist and to understand her role in history through a socialist lens—as she put it in "My Novitiate," to hope that "within the inevitable development of modern industry was the coming solution"—Kelley acted autonomously, making the fullest possible use of the social and political resources available to her, only one of which was the theory and practice of socialism. Nevertheless, socialist ideas exerted a deep and sustained influence on her thinking, providing Florence Kelley with a means of interpreting her personal and political relationship to the historical changes going on around her, and giving her an international standard by which to measure progress and change in her own society.

After graduating from Cornell in 1882, Kelley published two major undergraduate papers in the *International Review*, a New York periodical for which her father sometimes wrote. Those papers, "Must Our Working Women Despair?" and "The Legal History of the Child Since Blackstone," were both researched in the Library of Congress in Washington, D.C., where Florence lived with her father and worked independently during her last years at Cornell. However, in spite of her obvious qualifications, Kelley was not admitted to graduate study at the University of Pennsylvania "by reason of her gender," thereby frustrating her desires to put her education to some socially-constructive use, and making her keenly aware of the artificial limits her society placed on the use of women's talents.

In "My Novitiate," Kelley described her 1883 conversion to socialism in words similar to those used by nineteenth-century Evangelicals to describe their religious conversions from sin to redemption. Her mind "was tinder awaiting a match," and the match was the student socialist movement in Zurich. Thus Kelley's conversion to socialism involved more than an intellectual shift from one set of ideas to another. It also involved a change in her social position and a cultural switch from Anglo-American to European cultures, since in 1883 she married a Russian-Polish-Jewish medical student, who was also a socialist. For the next five years, her friends, political associates, and family life were shaped by German culture—first in Zurich, then in New York City, where Kelley and Wischnewetzky moved with their infant son in 1886, joining the German-speaking local chapter of the Socialist Labor Party. Between 1884 and 1887 Kelley gave birth to three children, during which time she also translated Friedrich Engel's classic work, *The Condition of the Working Class in England in 1844*, an investigative study based largely on government sources, such as factory-inspection and census reports.[5] In 1887, she arranged for its publication in English in New York. Kelley's extensive correspondence with Engels reflected her personal friendship as well as her business relationship with him—a friendship forged in London where the Wischnewetzky family visited the aging Engels on their way from Zurich to New York.

On her return, Kelley's 1887 article, "The Need of Theoretical Preparation for Philanthropic Work," was her declaration of independence from the palliative, stop-gap philanthropy traditionally undertaken by American women. It was also a call for "radical measures" from her generation of young, college-educated women. Written at a time when Kelley thought of herself as a translator, distributor and publicist of the writings of Marx, Engels and other scientific socialists, her article explained that:

The appropriation of the surplus value created by the workers is the real cause of the need of any philanthropic work. If they were not ground down by competition to the bare means of subsistence, plundered systematically of the fruits of their labor, they would not furnish social wreckage, as they are now doomed to do.

The need for theoretical study resulted, Kelley wrote, from the fact that:

any radical measures directed against this profit-plunder are measures directly against the class that lives by it; and to that class we belong by birth, and especially by education.

These views put Kelley in the vanguard of her generation as a critic of traditional charitible activity. Her perspective was decidedly that of a radical who made "common cause" with the working class.

Very soon after writing this article Kelley (and her husband) were expelled from the New York Socialist Labor Party. Her letters to

Engels make it clear that regardless of the charges about her use of party funds, the real reason for the expulsion was Kelley's ongoing challenge to the intellectual status quo of the SLP. As she wrote in December, 1887:

> It is pitiful to see *Capital* and *die Lage* persistently kept dark, while *the Sozialist* forces Rosenberg's *Tantalus* into the foreground week by week and the *Volkszeitung* devotes column-long articles to puffing such a mediocre production as Gronlund's *Caira* or *Danton in the French Revolution*....
> This confused stuff is puffed to the skies by the German Socialist press here, in the face of shameful neglect of the now accessible literature of scientific-materialistic criticism.[6]

Kelley was reinstated to membership by the national executive committee of the SLP later that year, but she had already shifted her intellectual and political interests away from the translation and distribution of English translations of "scientific-materialistic criticism" toward what was to be a lifelong interest in labor legislation for women and children. As she wrote Engels in March, 1888:

> I am working up the subject of Child Labor (and Compulsory Education) using statistics of State Bureaus, State Board of Education reports, census, Factory Inspectors reports, etc.[7]

Thus Kelley paid Engels the compliment of imitating his 1844 writings on England.

From 1888 to 1892 Kelley was in transition from the male-dominated world of the Socialist Labor Party to the female-dominated world of women's reform organizations. This transition moved Kelley from theory to practice, from the reform style of an intellectual to that of a social worker. While she could not claim to be making common cause with the working class to end the competitive, "profit-plunder" system, neither was she engaged in meaningless philanthropy, for her goals were permanently to alter factory conditions, not merely to send a few child workers to the country for recreation.

By February, 1891, Kelley was engaged in collective political action with other women on behalf of child labor legislation in New York, noting in a letter to Richard T. Ely:

We have a bill in the legislature for placing messenger boys
and cash girls under the factory acts and reducing the working
day of minors to eight hours.[8]

Although the "we" in this letter remains obscure, Kelley almost
certainly meant the New York Consumers League, the first of its
kind, which began under the direction of Josephine Shaw Lowell in
1890. Later, under Kelley's leadership as General Secretary from its
founding in 1898 till her death in 1932, the National Consumers
League and its local affiliates grew dramatically in numbers and
strength. By 1908 they had become the single most important
political force behind the passage and enforcement of labor legislation for women and children at both the state and Federal levels.

Kelley's relationship with her husband deteriorated in the early
1890s, and in December 1891 she moved to Chicago. There she
became a resident of Hull House, her children joining the
household of reformer Henry Demarest Lloyd in nearby Winnetka.

During her eight years of collective living with Jane Addams,
Julia Lathrop, and other talented women reformers of her generation in Chicago, Kelley remained firmly committed to socialism as
a personal belief system. To Richard T. Ely, Professor of
Economics at the University of Wisconsin in 1894, when she was at
the height of her political influence in Chicago as Chief Factory Inspector for the State of Illinois, she wrote:

I personally participate in the work of social reform because
part of it develops along Socialist lines, and part is an absolutely necessary protest against the brutalizing of us all by
Capitalism. Not because our Hull-House work alone would
satisfy me.[9]

Doubtless one important source for Kelley's sustained commitment
to socialism during the 1890's was the receptivity to socialist ideas
she found among middle-class Chicagoans. As she wrote to Engels:

The increased discussion of socialism here is very marked,
though the study of books and requests for lectures come
almost exclusively from people of the prosperous middle
classes. Thus I have been asked to speak twice before the
Secular Union and five times in churches in Chicago and its
suburbs, and the more radically I speak the more vigorous the
discussion in all these meetings.[10]

Thus Kelley was one of many middle-class Americans who were actively considering alternatives to the contemporary rule of *laissez-faire* capitalism.

Similarly, Kelley's ongoing commitment to socialism was sustained by the support her reform efforts received from her colleagues at Hull House, the first of two social settlements in which Kelley lived collectively with other women from 1891 to 1926. (After returning to New York in 1898 as the General Secretary of the National Consumers' League, Kelley lived in Lillian Wald's Nurses Settlement on Henry Street on the lower East Side until 1926). Of Hull House Kelley wrote to Engels in April 1892:

> I am conducting a bureau of women's labor and learning more in a week, of the actual conditions of proletarian life in America than any previous year.

> We have a colony of efficient and intelligent women living in a working men's quarter with the house used for all sorts of purposes by about a thousand persons a week. The last form of its activity is the formation of unions of which we have three, the cloak-makers, the shift makers, and the book-binders. Next week we are to take the initiative in the systematic endeavor to clean out the sweating dens... The Trades Assembly is paying the expenses of weekly mass meetings; and the sanitary authorities are emphasizing the impossibility of their coping, unaided, with the task allotted to them. So we may expect some more palliative measures pretty soon.[11]

Hull House provided Kelley with an institutional base for collective political action—action that she saw as "along socialist lines," even though she also recognized its limitations..

Kelley's appointment as the first Chief Factory Inspector of Illinois by reform governor John Peter Altgeld in 1893 allowed her to construct her own staff of twelve—five of whom, the legislation specified, had to be women. As she wrote Engels in 1893:

> I find my work as inspector most interesting; and as Governor Altgeld places no restrictions whatever upon our freedom of speech, and the English etiquette of silence while in the civil

service is unknown here, we are not hampered by our position and three of my deputies and my assistant are outspoken Socialists and active in agitation.[12]

By 1894, through her effective enforcement of the eight-hour-day for women and children (legislation she had helped draft in 1893), Kelley had produced a major victory in industrial practice. As she wrote Engels on New Year's Eve, 1894:

> We have at last won a victory for our 8-hours law. The Supreme Court has handed down no decision sustaining it, but the stockyards magnates having been arrested until they are tired of it, have instituted the 8-hours day for 10,000 employees, men, women and children. We have 18 suits pending to enforce the 8-hours law and we think we shall establish it permanently before Easter.[13]

Thus Kelley struck a powerful, if temporary, blow for the eight-hour-day—one of the most popular goals of the American labor movement from 1880 to 1930. However, Kelley's efforts were stymied by the legal challenges of the Illinois Association of Manufacturers, which was founded in 1894 for the sole purpose of gaining the law's repeal. This they accomplished in 1895.[14]

A personal friend of Eugene V. Debs, Kelley joined the Socialist Party of America soon after its founding and apparently remained a member throughout the decade before World War I —years when the Socialist Party enjoyed unparalleled electoral success. In 1913 in an exchange of letters with the Executive Director of the New York chapter of the party, Kelley showed that while she remained independent in her thinking and action, she also viewed herself as a loyal party member. Noting that she had been reported in the newspapers as endorsing a Democratic candidate for an appeals judge election when a Socialist candidate was also running, the party official wrote asking her for an explanation, warning that she might be "guilty of violating the Constitution of the Party." She replied at length, providing detailed reasons why her absence from New York caused her to be unaware of the Socialist Party candidate, and explained that her desire to unseat a bad judge and elect a good one had caused her to overlook "all other considerations." Accepting the notion of party discipline, Kelley concluded:

In my eager desire for the defeat of Judge Werner, I never
thought of the rule of the Party which I considered a
necessary rule (in spite of having broken it through forget-
fulness on this occasion) that members must not promote the
election of candidates of other parties.[15]

Thus while Kelley's independent political base with the National
Consumers League naturally produced independent political action
on her part, her intellectual and political allegiance to socialism
remained intact.

After 1900, however, Kelley's chief institutional activity within
organized socialism was not with the Socialist Party itself, but with
socialist youth organizations, such as the Intercollegiate Socialist
Society and the League for Industrial Democracy. Kelley served as
a Vice-President of the Intercollegiate Socialist Society for many
years, representing Cornell.[16] During the first two decades of the
twentieth century she was a frequent speaker on American
campuses—especially at elite Eastern institutions, where she
recruited able young people to carry on her reform work. One such
recruit was Frances Perkins (Secretary of Labor under President
Franklin Roosevelt in the 1930s) who decided to work with Kelley
and pursue a career in reform after hearing her speak at Mount
Holyoke College in 1902.[17]

By 1923, when the FBI began to keep a file on her, Kelley was
well-known to generations of socialist students as a charismatic
speaker. Filed under "The Youth Movement in America," Kelley's
FBI report identified her as a "speaker for the Harvard Liberal
Club [who] has been a radical all the sixty-four years of her life, it
seems," and noted, "She was one of the much-applauded speakers
at the meeting of the Trade Union Educational League in
Washington in May, and at the June Conference of the League for
Industrial Democracy at Camp Tamiment."[18] Kelley came to the
FBI's attention through her scathing denunciations of the U.S.
Supreme Court, since the Court in 1923 in Adkins v. Children's
Hospital declared the District of Columbia minimum-wage law for
women unconstitutional, thereby calling into question the legal
basis on which much of Kelley's work stood—the assumption that
state and Federal courts would accept the legality of protective

labor legislation limiting hours and specifying minimum wages for women even though they would not accept such laws for men.

Unfortunately she did not live long enough to see many of her ideas become part of New Deal legislation in the 1930s—particularly the 1938 Fair Labor Standards Act, which established an eight-hour-day and minimum wages for both men and women workers, and the Social Security Act of 1935, with its provisions for federal funding for aid to poor families with dependent children. Ending just when she emerged as a national figure around 1900, her memoirs addressed questions related to the origins of her reform motivation rather than questions about the consequences of her career, but her narrative's frequent references to current political struggles revealed her assumptions about the importance of what she and other women reformers had achieved after thirty years of collective effort.

From an early age Kelley was keenly aware of the brutalizing possibilities of industrial capitalism, and she saw her reform work as an effort to reduce that brutality, especially in the lives of women and children workers, through labor legislation enacted and enforced by the state. Throughout her career, the socialist ideals of Kelley's youth remained with her as a guiding, if not a definitive force, in her thought and action. While Kelley's incomplete depiction of her experience as a socialist narrows the scope of what we learn from her memoirs about her life, it does not invalidate them as an accurate source of information. She developed her own national power base in the National Consumers League after 1900, and as early as 1890 organized socialism had become a peripheral rather than a central feature of her political landscape. Thus its omission from this brief autobiography does not injure the integrity of her account.

Perhaps the greatest loss attached to Kelley's self-censorship was that it deprived her of the opportunity to tell her readers why her personal sense of herself as a socialist was such an important part of her private identity, shaping her sense of herself as a reformer at Hull House in the 1890s and of her obligations as a citizen in New York in 1913. Like many autobiographies, including the classic among her contemporaries, Jane Addams' *Twenty Years at Hull*

House (1910), Kelley's reminiscences did not reveal her personal life, though they take us to the threshold and make us wish we could enter.

Her correspondence shows that there was more to Kelley's life than appears in this brief account. Nevertheless, her memoirs give us one of our most dramatic glimpses into the emerging reform world of the 1880s and 1890s, and they demonstrate how women gained access to leadership in that world by constructing their own institutions.

Kathryn Kish Sklar

Los Angeles, California
June, 1985

Notes

This introduction draws on research on Florence Kelley undertaken with the assistance of the Newberry Library, Chicago, with a fellowship from the National Endowment for the Humanities, and with the help of earlier fellowships from The Rockefeller Foundation, the Woodrow Wilson International Center for Scholars in Washington, D.C., the Schlesinger Library for the History of Women in the United States, Cambridge, Massachusetts, and the Faculty Senate of U.C.L.A. I am grateful for this support. I am also grateful for the expert research assistance in Chicago of Lynn I. Weiner, and at the University of California, Los Angeles, for the able assistance of Beth Weisz-Buck and Nan Yamane.

¹ The first in Kelley's series, "My Philadelphia," was the lead article in *The Survey Graphic*, Vol. LVII, No. 1 (October 1, 1926). Others were published subsequently in Vol. LVIII, (1927): "When Co-Education was Young," (Feb. 1); "My Novitiate," (April 1); and "I Go to Work," (June 1). For a study of the magazine's place in Progressive reform, see Clarke A Chambers, *Paul V. Kellogg and The Survey: Voices for Social Welfare and Social Justice* (Minneapolis: University of Minnesota Press, 1971).

Kelley was for many years an Associate Editor of *Survey*. The demands of Kelley's schedule were indicated by the rate at which her writings on other topics continued to be published during the eight months that her autobiographical articles were appearing in *Survey* October 1926-June 1927. During those months the magazine also published the following by Kelley: one article, "The Sheppard-Towner Act," (Feb. 15); one review, "The New Challenges of Child Labor," (Feb. 15); three editorials, "Montana Ratifies the Child Labor Amendment" (March 1); "Arkansas Admitted to the Birth Registration Era" (March 15); "Maryland and Missouri," (May 15); and a letter, "Child Labor in Massachusetts" (April 15). During this time Kelley also published other articles, including "Children's Compensation for Industrial Injuries," in *Public Health Nurse*, Vol. 19 (June 1927). Thus her *Notes of Sixty Years* was part of a larger schedule of writing, speaking, and administrating.

² Felix Frankfurter, "Foreword" in Josephine Goldmark, *Impatient Crusader: Florence Kelley's Life Story* (Westport, Connecticut: Greenwood Press, 1976 reprint of 1953 original). Goldmark's book focuses on Kelley's career after 1900. For other studies of Kelley, see Dorothy Rose Blumberg, *Florence Kelley: The Making of a Social Pioneer* (N.Y.: Augustus Kelley, 1966); which emphasizes Kelley's career before 1900; Doroth Rose Blumberg, "Dear Mr. Engels: Unpublished Letters of Florence Kelley (Wisnewetzky) to Friedrich Engels, 1884-1894," *Labor History* (Spring 1964); and Louise Wade, "Florence Kelley," in *Notable American Women*, Edward James, Janet James and Paul Boyer, Eds., (Cambridge, Massachusetts: Harvard University Press, 1971), Vol. II.

³ A valuable work on the "red scare" is William Preston, Jr., *Aliens and Dissenters: Federal Suppression of Radicals, 1903-1933* (Cambridge: Harvard University Press, 1963). For the social settlement movement, see Allen F. Davis, *Spearheads for Reform: The Social Settlement Movement and the Progressive Party, 1890-1915* (N.Y.: Oxford University Press, 1967)

⁴ The major work on the history of American women and socialism is Mari Jo Buhle, *Women and American Socialism* (Urbana: University of Illinois Press, 1979). See also Salley M. Miller, *Flawed Liberation: Socialism and Feminism* (Westport, Connecticut: Greenwood Press, 1981), and

Philip S. Foner and Sally M. Miller, *Kate Richards O'Hare: Selected Writings and Speeches* (Baton Rouge: Louisiana State University Press, 1982). Another pertinent study is Oakley C. Johnson, *Marxism in the United States History Before the Russian Revolution (1876-1917)* (New York: Humanities Press, 1974).

[5] Until 1958 Kelley's was the only English translation of this important book. For a recent paperback edition using Kelley's translation, see Eric Hobsbawm, Ed., Friedrich Engels, *The Condition of the Working Class in England in 1844* (England: Grenada, 1979 reprint).

[6] Florence Kelley to Friedrich Engels, New York, Dec. 29, 1887. Archive, Institute of Marxism-Leninism, No. 4798. I am grateful to Dorothy Rose Blumberg for sharing her copy of this microfilm with me.

[7] Florence Kelley to Friedrich Engels, N.Y., March 29, 1888, Archive, Institute of Marxism-Leninism, No. 11836.

[8] Florence Kelley to Richard Ely, New York, Feb., 1891. Richard Ely Papers, State Historical Society of Wisconsin, Madison, Wisconsin.

[9] Florence Kelley to Richard Ely, Chicago, June 21, 1891

[10] Florence Kelley to Friedrich Engels, Chicago, Hull House, Nov. 27, 1892. Archive No. 8491.

[11] Florence Kelley to Friedrich Engels, Hull House, April 7, 1892, Archive No. 8490.

[12] *Ibid.*

[13] Florence Kelley to Friedrich Engels, Chicago, Dec. 31, 1894. Archive, No. 8494. For the eight-hour day movement, see David Roediger and Philip S. Foner, *American Labor and the Shorter Working Day: A History*, forthcoming. Kelley's early struggles on behalf of such labor legislation for women and children from 1890 to 1930 set precedents for the passage of legislation that applied to men as well, especially the Fair Labor Standards Act of 1938. For a variety of historical reasons, such labor legislation was strongly endorsed by trade unions in Britain, but in the US it was not. Therefore it fell to women's organizations to advance this legislation in the US, while in Britain it was advanced by male organizations, including the Liberal and Labour Parties.

Scholars who study the history of women in the United States have tended to take a hostile view of this argument, since such "protective" labor legislation for women was used in the 1920s to exclude some women from well-paying jobs and preserve these jobs for men. Historians have not yet assessed the effect of these protective laws on most women workers, but a recent sociological study has examined the historical data from the Progressive Era and concluded that these protective laws benefitted women workers much more than they harmed them. See Ronnie Steinberg, *Wages and Hours: Labor and Reform in Twentieth-Century America* (New Bruswick: Rutgers University Press, 1982).

Historical thinking about this topic has been shaped by the recent struggle for the Equal Rights Amendment in which the justness of the ERA has blinded many of its supporters, including historians, to its class origins in the 1920s among professional women, and to the damage it would have done to recent improvements in working conditions for women. For these reasons the overwhelming majority of women's organizations and women's unions were against the ERA, Kelley leading them in the name of justice for working women.

[14] See Alfred Kelley, "The History of the Illinois Manufacturers Association," Ph.D. diss., University of Chicago, 1939.

[15] J. Gerber to Florence Kelley, Nov. 15, 1913, and Florence Kelley to Comrade Gerber, Fayetteville, N.Y., Nov. 21, 1913. Socialist Party Papers, Local New York, Letter Books, 1907-1914, Microfilm, Tamiment Library, New York University.

[16] See Max Horn, "The Intercollegiate Socialist Society, 1905-1921: Origins of the Modern Student Movement," PhD dissertation, Columbia University, 1975.

[17] Charles H. Trout, "Frances Perkins," *Notable American Women: The Modern Period*, Barbara Sicherman, et. al, Eds., (Cambridge: Harvard University Press, 1980).

[18] Florence Kelley's unpaginated Federal Bureau of Investigation file was obtained through the U.S. Freedom of Information Act.

1892.

Working People's Social
Science Club, Hull House, 335
So. Halsted St. meets Tues-
days at 8 O'clock P.M.

A speech of 45 minutes is
followed by a discussion.

PROGRAM.

Feb. 2,   "Child Labor"
  Mrs. Florence Kelley.
Feb. 9, "Our Jury System",
  Sigmund Zeisler.
Feb. 16, "The Chicago Police"
  Major R.W. McClaughry.
Feb. 23, "The Cook County
   House of Correction"
  Mr. Mark Crawford.
Mar. I,   "Competition"
  Col. Aldace F. Walker.
Mar. 8, "The Cook Co. Courts"
  Judge M. F. Tuley.
Mar. 15, "The Municipal Con-
   trol of Heat, Light,
   and Transportation"
  Col. Augustus Jacobson.

HULL-HOUSE SOCIAL SCIENCE CLUB PROGRAM, 1892

The
Autobiography
Of
Florence Kelley

HULL-HOUSE

FLORENCE KELLEY AS A CHILD

My Philadelphia

My earliest dated mental picture has to do with the death of President Lincoln. I was five years old, visiting my grandparents in Germantown, then a suburb of Philadelphia. They lived in an ivy-clad, pebble-dashed, gable-roofed old house, on a slightly terraced hillside, overlooking the lovely little Wingohocking Creek, long since, alas! become a city sewer.

At the foot of the terrace was a goldfish pond. Hector, the big Newfoundland dog, was waiting for me below my window as I dressed for breakfast. It was a sunny day, and a robin ran over the close-cropped, bright green grass of the back garden. Nothing could have been gayer.

How different the breakfast table! My taciturn grandfather's formidable features (so like President Jackson's that I had never doubted that the two-cent postage-stamps of the time were family portraits of our own) looked that day as if chiseled in stone. My grandmother, serene in all my previous experience of her, looked shattered, and was silent throughout the meal. After breakfast she said to me:

"In times of grief it is well for families to be together. You and I will drive to your home." Then in a voice of utter sadness she added:

"My child, President Lincoln is dead. He was shot last night."

We drove in silence the seven miles to our parents' home in West Philadelphia. The sidewalks were empty. People were draping their doors with mourning, and shutters were closed as if Death had entered every home. In the study my mother was sewing deep mourning on the flag that had been so often raised to celebrate victories during the war.

Father was not at home because he had gone several days before, as one of the guests of the Government, asked to rear again the flag of the Union over the ruins of Fort Sumter. I have before me the faded copy of a Philadelphia newspaper of a fortnight later which reported a speech he made before the girls' High and Normal School. In this he told how the news had reached them:

"Upon the good ship *Arago* the Army and Navy were represented by distinguished officers, judges of the Supreme Court of the United States and of some of the States, members of both Houses of Congress, some of the most distinguished lights of the pulpit, the bar and the universities. It was a goodly and pleasant company.

"Leaving Hilton Head we were nearing Fort Sumter, when a steamer approached and General Gilmore called to us that Lee had surrendered, and that he had with him the particulars of the terms of surrender.

"A few hours later the prow of our vessel was turned homeward. All was bright and beautiful and cheerful. We were off Cape Henry, looking out for Fortress Monroe, when a little boat passed close to our stern. He who held its helm cried:

" 'Why is not your flag at half mast? Have you not heard of the President's death?'

"That was the first intimation we had received of the dreadful occurence. We refused to credit it; we could not credit it. We looked into each other's faces and were silent."

Because I was so little I was, of course, left at home on the day of the funeral services at Independence Hall (April 23) where President Lincoln's body was brought to Philadelphia from Washington on its way to Springfield; but an older brother, William Darrah Kelley, recalls the formal occurrences of that day and writes of the city "hushed and draped in black" and the great crowds which thronged in front of the historic building.

Only a little later in memory came Father's first contribution to the strange, incoherent process of my education. Of all the things he told me in early childhood, only one left a deeper impression than this: That the duty of his generation was to build up great industries in America so that more wealth could be produced for the whole people. "The duty of your generation," he often said, "will be to see that the product is distributed justly. The same generation cannot do both."

William Darrah Kelley, our father, was almost thirty years continuously a member of the House of Representatives in Washington and was known towards the close of that long service as the Father of the House. He had run for Congress in 1856 with Fremont, on the Free Soil ticket, and at a critical time in the convention of the new Republican Party in Chicago in 1860 his long and impressive speech had the attention of the delegates until the committee brought in Lincoln's nomination. Father was chosen by the Pennsylvania group as their representative on the committee which visited Mr. Lincoln to notify him of his nomination. Father was himself elected to the House of Representatives that November, 1860, and first took his seat at the extra session called on July 4, 1861. He was reelected fourteen times consecutively, and was a member of the House at the time of his death, in January, 1890, representing always the Fourth Congressional District of Pennsylvania.

Throughout the long period of his service in Congress his dominant, absorbing passion was the development of the natural resources of our country, primarily those of Pennsylvania.

Although as a Member of Congress Father was exempt from service in the Civil War, he volunteered and, when Pennsylvania was threatened by the Confederate Army, he went out with the Reserves. His huge musket and light blue army overcoat and cap greatly impressed us even when they hung in a closet long after the war.

On my tenth birthday in 1869, Father was at home because it fell in one of his long vacations, which gave, in alternate years between the long and short sessions, abundant time for travel and for inquiring into the practical effects of tariff duties upon manufacturing industries, many of which were, in the years immediately following the Civil War, still "infants."

On this memorable birthday I was reading, on the floor of the study, a delightfully illustrated volume entitled *The Resources of California*, which Father had brought back from a journey thither.

He had been a member of the Committee of Ways and Means which earlier that year had gone to Promontory Point, Utah, to see the famous "Golden Spike" driven home, which united the eastern and western halves of the first transcontinental railroad and had continued their journey to the Pacific coast. Finding me absorbed in the text as well as pictures, he welcomed me with enthusiasm into a companionship which has enriched my whole life.

Because I never went regularly to school, and encouraged by his 'interest I began then, at the age of ten years and wholly without guidance, to read Father's library through, starting at the ceiling, at the southwest corner of the study and continuing the process whenever we were at home until, at the age of seventeen, I entered Cornell University.

Father had taught me to read when I was seven years old, in a terrible little book with woodcuts of children no older than myself, balancing with their arms heavy loads of wet clay on their heads, in brickyards in England. They looked like little gnomes and trolls, with crooked legs, and splay feet large out of all proportion to their dwarfed frames. The text told of the hardships they were then suffering, nearly two decades after Lord Shaftesbury's bill to shorten the working hours of women and children in English factories had been enacted by Parliament. When my mother and grandmother remonstrated with him for darkening the mind of a young child with such dismal ideas, he replied seriously that life can never be right for all the children until the cherished boys and girls are taught to know the facts in the lives of their less fortunate contemporaries.

In after years, and as my work of factory inspector and advocate of labor laws took me to the sweatshops and milltowns of the industrial states, other images were to take their place beside these, images which stood out against backgrounds of garment factory and textile mill, machine shop and foundry with the poignant appeal of human flesh and blood. But my pictures of exploited children always ranged back to these boys and girls of the English industrial revolution which had preceded ours, and the vividness with which my father had described the children's plight.

Father told me of slave children who, born after I was and down to President Lincoln's Proclamation of Emancipation, had been sold away from their parents to grow up in distant states, far from their brothers and sisters. He had talked about children in his own generation called "bound" boys and "bound" girls, who came from England under indenture to the people who brought them. They had to work long years without wages as household servants or unskilled farm help, to pay the costs of their journey to the land of the free.

To Father's mind these toiling English children were living evidence of the evils of Free Trade. He felt profoundly the evil of promulgating, for our new industry, the theory of *laissez faire*. He believed in forty acres and a mule for freedmen, homesteads for immigrants, and tariffs for American manufacture. To my generation, other measures commended themselves and became my burning concern; but Father's charge had been to meet the issues of the ensuing decades with such light as might be ours.

In his study, from which I was never willingly absent when he was at home, and in long walks together after that fortunate birthday, there was always in his mind the leaven of the idea of a juster, nobler, happier life for all the American people once a firm industrial foundation, as he saw it, had been laid.

Father's never failing, flowing interest in the misfortunes of defenseless women and children arose in part from his early experiences. He was born in Philadelphia in 1814, the youngest of four children, his three elders being sisters. His earliest clear recollection was of sitting on the lowest step of the stairs, by the open front door of his home, while his sister brushed the white marble steps, singing at the top of her voices:

> *There is a Fountain filled with blood*
> *Drawn from Immanuel's veins.*

As she finished the second line he ran out and down the street, calling back to her, "I don't want to hear about blood." That was the earliest recorded protest in his long life of protest and dissent.

While I was still a little girl, he told me the story of his mother's experience immediately following his father's death in 1816. There was then no lien law exempting for widows and their orphan children any remnants of possessions wherewith to begin life anew, no law protecting them from loss of the tools of the father's trade nor of the meagerest necessities of dependent children. There were no widows' pensions, no mothers' allowances, no scholarships payable out of taxes.

The family had been prosperous until my grandfather David

Kelley, a leading jeweler in Philadelphia, indorsed the note of a brother-in-law, who long survived him, but whose failure to meet this note caused him to lose his business and his life. Grandfather Kelley died of apoplexy at the age of thirty-two years, when Father was two years old.

Out of that early prosperity there remained at his death household silver, christening cups and porridge spoons, glass, china and linen, besides the larger furniture. These were to be sold at auction on a certain day by the holders of Grandfather's signature to the note. The family treasurers were spread on tables, and the intending bidders were beginning to gather when a substantial looking member of the Society of Friends appeared with a large basket on each arm. She quickly filled her baskets with desirable objects of manageable size, and went her way, remarking to those who looked on: "It seems strange that Friend Hannah Kelley should not have returned precious heirlooms." She was known to several persons present and her undoubted respectability prevented any attempt to interfere with her departure. Many weeks later the Friend returned with her baskets saying, according to family tradition: "Thee will have abundant use, Friend Kelley, for these belongings for thyself and thy children. I feel sure that thee has not misconstrued my good intention."

Sectarian differences in those days were no less than they are now, and our grandparents were Presbyterian. The name of this truly Friendly neighbor has been handed down in the family, with the story of her practical protest against a law which gave to the creditor everything belonging to the deceased, and gave to his widow and orphaned children nothing.

Although he was too young to remember the episode of Friend Scattergood, the subsequent hardships experienced by his mother and her brood made a lifelong impression upon Father. This auction was often mentioned in his early childhood, and contributed to his perennial interest in measures intended to protect women and children by statute, by legal interpretation, and by enfranchising women.

With some help from her husband's brother, my grandmother managed to keep her brood together. But times continued hard long after the War of 1812, and at the age of eleven, Father was obliged to go to work as errand-boy in a printing house. From November until May his hours of work were from 6 a.m. to 8 p.m.;

from May until November they were from light until dark. This beloved little only son found it impossible to keep awake toward the end of his working day, and a friendly printer told him to bring some green tea leaves and chew them as he worked. Father attributed the nervous excitability which distressed him throughout his long life to those early years of strain and fatigue. Here, much nearer home than English brickyards, I had a glimpse of the lot of less fortunate children.

Our earliest known ancestor was Thomas Kelley, first of three generations of Thomases. A Protestant from the North of Ireland, he sailed up the Delaware in 1662, and his son acquired some landed possession on the New Jersey side at a place now impossible to locate, but then known as Ruff's Landing. The line is straight and has been traced from that original Thomas Kelley of 1662 through John Kelley of Salem, New Jersey, who was a major in the Revolution, to his descendant, David Kelley (1784-1816), the Philadelphia jeweler, who was our father's father. All the known Kelleys of this line hailed from Londonderry, Ireland, except David Kelley's mother, Father's grandmother, Elizabeth Casteau, daughter of a Huguenot family, long settled in New Jersey.

To this respectable genealogy Father's mother, Hannah Darrah, added the record of her father, William Darrah, an officer in the French and Indian wars, and in the Revolution. He received eight hundred acres of land in Bucks County, Pennsylvania, as reward of his service in the earlier wars. In the Civil War, the family was represented by Father and our mother's two brothers, Henry W. and William R. Bonsall.

We are thus descended from people, Irish, English and Huguenot, who came to America to escape oppression, and to find freedom of worship and, as it turned out, to found families destined honorably to hold their own in the professions, in business and in the Government.

Childhood free as sunshine from fear of punishment, rebuke or criticism, was rare in the period between 1859 and 1870, yet such a childhood was mine to the age of eleven years. Conviction of sin was far, indeed, from our knowledge.

Father had been identified with the first Unitarian Church in Philadelphia of which William H. Furness was pastor for more than a half century. Dr. Furness had married my parents in 1854, and participated in the service at Father's funeral in 1890. It was a source of lasting satisfaction that shortly before the Civil War, when a meeting of the church members was held to consider a recent anti-slavery sermon delivered by Dr. Furness, Father spoke strongly in his support and for the anti-slavery cause. There was no censure of the sermon.

On the fringe of my childhood moved numerous aunts of assorted religious beliefs—Baptist, Episcopalian, Presbyterian. Out of all this variety there could obviously crystallize in my mind no fear of Hell-fire or eternal punishment of any kind. Indeed, I can truly say that in those tender years I knew no fear except of my colored mammy's ghost stories until (when I was eleven years old) the loss of my fifth and last surviving sister robbed the sunshine of its glory and created a shadow lasting to this present day. But I was then too young to share Mother's permanent terror of impending loss. Our mother's own parents had died in her early childhood. Her two brothers had died (one at our home) of lingering tuberculosis following service in the Civil War. Uncle William Bonsall served as a surgeon. Four of my little sisters had died in infancy, and this fifth loss of a daughter who had almost reached her seventh birthday brought to my mother, who survived her more than thirty years, a settled, gentle melancholy which she could only partly disguise for the sake of my two brothers and myself, her only surviving daughter.

Even conscientious adherence to the rule of the Society of Friends that Death, being a part of the Divine order of nature, should not be followed by mourning apparel or darkening of the home, brought only outward cheerfulness. Our home was, however, kept filled with young people. Indeed during the years when my brothers were students at the University of Pennsylvania, the breakfast table was never without an extra place for the young friend whom each was free to bring home over night without notice and it was characteristic of our mother's utter unselfishness that she assented to my going to Cornell, because I should there have abundant young companionship which my early childhood had so lacked.

I was the third of eight children, all fine, healthy boys and girls, of whom all but three died in infancy and early childhood from infections now universally recognized as preventable and actually prevented more effectually every year.

After the death in 1859, of my elder sister Elizabeth, aged two years, entries in the family Bible followed with pitiful frequency. There were, all told, five in twelve years: Marian in 1863, aged eleven months; Josephine in 1865, aged seven months; Caroline in 1869, aged four months; and Anna in 1871, aged six years.

All this grief, this anguish of frustrated hope occurred, not on the plains as a hardship of pioneer life, not in the Great American Desert where physicians were out of reach, but within four miles of Independence Hall, in one of the great and famous cities of the Nineteenth Century. These tenderly cherished young lives were sacrificed, not to the will of God, as mothers were taught throughout the long history of the race but, as we know now, to the prevailing ignorance of the hygiene of infancy.

As late as 1918 our Republic was laggard in the care of mothers and young children. We were number ten among the nations when measured by our infant deathrate. With great joy, therefore, I recognized that a new day had dawned and that, sooner or later, there would be an end to the nation wide tragedy of mothers bereft of their young children. For in July of that year Jeannette Rankin of Montana, the first woman member of Congress, introduced in the House of Representatives her bill for an appropriation by Congress to be distributed among the states, and by them administered in cooperation with the Children's Bureau of the United States Department of Labor. Three years later this bill, first known as the Rankin-Robinson bill and afterward as the Sheppard-Towner Act, was passed by Congress, and signed by President Harding on November 23, 1921.

For four years this life-saving measure has been administered with extraordinary intelligence and success by the Children's Bureau cooperating with the state health departments. Under its stimulus, public health nurses have been introduced in hundreds of counties where they had hardly been heard of. Clinics and classes for mothers and little children have been spread over backward states many of which, four years ago, had appallingly high death rates. State boards of health publish with pride the falling infant death rates, and stir in turn the professional pride of local officials and voluntary associations in this beneficent rivalry.

Of all the activities in which I have shared during more than forty years of striving, none is, I am convinced, of such fundamental importance as the Sheppard-Towner Act. It establishes the principle that the Republic shares with each state responsibility for the life and health of the children. Under it death rates are showing a downward trend, educational provisions under medical guidance are spreading, many of the fatal infections of childhood are increasingly controlled. Lonely ranches in Arizona and Idaho and slum dwellers in the most congested cities are increasingly able to command resources for safety of their young children, undreamed of by women of my mother's generation. Forty-three states and Hawaii are cooperating, all the states except Connecticut, Illinois, Kansas, Maine and Massachusetts.

My own modest share in this life-saving measure is an abiding happy memory. When the Children's Bureau bill passed in 1912, I was consulted among its advocates as to the order in which the subjects assigned to the Bureau for inquiry should be taken up. I urged immediate study of infant mortality. Sir Arthur Newsholme's monumental volume, then recent, pointed the way, and revealed by contrast this Republic's deplorable ignorance concerning our young children. An admirable series of Infant Mortality Studies followed. By 1918, a foundation of facts had been made available by the Children's Bureau for the use of Congress, which carried conviction and greatly expedited the passage of the Sheppard-Towner Act in 1921.

That Act is threatened with destruction. Congress adjourned in July [1926] without voting the appropriation necessary to its continuance. The House voted to continue the Act for two years; the Senate Committee reported the bill favorably, but with an amendment which would authorize the appropriation for only one additional year, *i.e.*, to June 30, 1928. Supporters of the bill refused to accept this amendment. The measure was debated on June 15, but did not come to a vote and is thus left on the calendar for the short session beginning in December. The biennial legislatures meeting in January will need to know how far Uncle Sam is continuing his cooperation with them, in order to meet his requirements intelligently in their own appropriations.

On July 8, Senator Bayard of Delaware sponsored in the *Congressional Record* thirty-five pages in support of charges that this life-saving measure and three others constitute a conspiracy for nationalizing American children. The other three measures are the Children's Bureau bill, the Federal Department of Education bill and the Child Labor amendment.

The *Congressional Record* is privileged. No suit, civil or criminal, can be brought against it. For libel and scurrility it is, therefore, a safe refuge and has been repeatedly so used in this long struggle for safety of life of the children who will be this Republic when present senators have gone to their reward.

The *Record* is so queer and dull that Senator Bayard's action would ordinarily be dismissed with the old joke that, when counsel for the defense has no case, he abuses the plaintiff's attorney. But this year one third of the Senators come up for election in November, and candidates were franking copies to their constituents as early as July, knowing that interest even in the *Record* is keen this year.

At this crisis in the history of the Sheppard-Towner Act it behooves the citizens of this country to ponder these questions:

Are we the billionaire miser among the nations?

When a family lets a sick child die and deliberately calls in no physician, a charge of manslaughter lies, and no plea of religious conviction or of dire poverty suffices. Do we as a people belong in that company?

If the opposition should triumph at the coming session as it did at the last one, if the authorization should not be renewed, if the Act be starved to death, shall we not stand revealed as too mean to keep alive helpless future citizens when we thus reject the methods that we, ourselves, have found effective wherever we have applied them, and that are used by all enlightened nations?

How does Congress propose to defend itself when voting mothers in all parts of the country ask again, as they did in 1919 and 1920, when the Sheppard-Towner bill was first pending, "Why does Congress wish babies to die?"

I should be false to the memory of a tender and grief-stricken mother if these pages were printed without reference to the need of action by Congress at the December Session.

Father built in 1850 a house in an ample square in West Philadelphia, four miles as the crow flies from Independence Hall, near what became, long after, Fairmount Park West. In that house I was born in September, 1859. It is now a hospital for women and children at Forty-first and Parrish Streets. The land had been a part of the estate of Judge Peters, and Father's plan was to participate in its development. He made his home there to the end of his life—forty years. Unfortunately the development lagged, and the story was often told in our family how, at Thanksgiving time, while I was a babe in arms, Mother called the members of her household to the front windows to see a flock of turkeys being driven into town to market for the holiday. She foretold that this was the last moving object they would see passing our house before Easter; and time proved the prophecy correct.

In this isolated home as time went on, my great resource was the library in the study. I have mentioned how on my tenth birthday I began to make its acquaintance in good earnest.

The top shelf was filled chiefly with modestly bound, small volumes of the Family Library. Though I understood almost nothing in these books of so-called Natural Science, and there were no illustrations to help, I did learn the names of Newton, Galileo, Giordano Bruno, Kepler, Copernicus and a few other astronomers, chemists and physicists whom I thereafter revered indiscriminately, classing them all with Dr. Priestley, who was a friend of Benjamin Franklin and, as will presently appear, a hero of the family.

Walter Scott, in nine large volumes of bad print, stood on a high shelf and was early reached. He saw me well along through the year of my twelfth birthday, partly because we left home in September and did not return until the following spring. That winter the Library of Congress afforded Dickens and Thackeray, along with Miss Alcott and Horatio Alger.

At home there was little poetry beyond Shakespeare, Milton, Byron, Goldsmith and several anthologies dear to my memory. But there were long shelves of history. Full sets of the writings of President Madison and Daniel Webster's orations, and the histories of Bancroft, Prescott and Francis Parkman, alone must have weighed hundreds of pounds.

Emerson's essays and Dr. Channing's sermons midway down the shelves, were identified, by their dates, with Father's sojourn in Boston as a young jeweler specializing in enameling. Indeed, when a costly set of gold cups were ordered for the Imaum of Muscat, Father's skill brought his employer a gold medal from the Massachusetts Mechanic's Association. But his free time was given to these leaders of thought in New England.

Fortunately for me, Emerson, Channing, Burke, Carlyle, Godwin and Herbert Spencer were near the floor, and I was nearly fifteen when I arrived at them. Even later, I encountered the toughest nut in the whole library, and soon gave up the tall, soberly bound volume as hopelessly beyond me. This was the collected plays of Wycherley, Congreve and Farquhar. Later when the books were divided among us after our father's death, a brother examining this volume asked sternly:

"Didn't Father once say that you had read all these books?"

When I replied that I had read all but the law books he exclaimed:

"If he, or we, had known when you came to this one, you would have been stopped right there." No harm had been done, however, for that volume had floored me completely and had been abandoned.

Only the circumstance that I was a very lonely child deeply ashamed of having no school experience, and was thereby goaded to strive against my consequent ignorance by my own unguided efforts, could have kept me a work six years (nearly seven) upon this huge, indigestible, intellectual meal.

Our mother's maiden mane was Caroline Bartram Bonsall, and her best known Quaker ancestor was John Bartram, the botanist, whose famous garden is now Bartram Park in Philadelphia. John Bartram, with Benjamin Franklin and William Coleman, was third among the founders of the American Philosophical Society where he represented the science of Botany. He was also an explorer and a maker of beautiful maps.

On a stone in the front wall of his house, John Bartram chiseled his simple creed:

> *'Tis God alone, Almighty Lord*
> *The Holy One, by me adored*
> *John Bartram 1770*

He was one of the earliest emancipators of slaves in the colonies. To a friend he said: "With us they are now free with victuals and clothes, and all other privileges which white men enjoy."

On the death in 1838 of our maternal grandfather, Henry L. Bonsall, a direct descendant of John Bartram, his little daughter Caroline whose mother had died five years before became by adoption (but retaining her name), the daughter of Isaac and Elizabeth Kay Pugh, who had been dear friends and neighbors of her parents.

Their peaceful home in Germantown, of which my earliest recollection was darkened by the death of President Lincoln, is to this day my ideal. Having none of their own they gathered in four little girls, of whom two were, like my mother, orphans. Never were father and mother more tenderly loved by children of their own flesh and blood than these.

Serene as was the daily life of this delightful home, it was animated by vital and lasting intellectual activities, rooted far back in England and America. Our grandmother, Elizabeth Kay Pugh, was born in a family of Unitarians, who came from England with Joseph Priestley, the chemist and Non-Conformist minister. In 1791, his chapel had been burned and his house sacked by a mob at Fairfield, Birmingham. He and his family escaped, but his material possessions and the records of chemical experiments, the labor of years, were annihilated. Going to London, he became preacher at Gravel Pit Chapel, Hackney, until 1794, when with his wife he emigrated to America. Sailing by the same vessel, as friends and sympathizers, were the parents and family of Elizabeth Kay.

Isaac Pugh, husband of Elizabeth Kay, was born in Pennsylvania in 1799, and was educated at Westtown Friends' Boarding School. When late in life he became blind, he talked to us with pleasure of his school days there. The Society of Friends was perfectly consistent in educating children according to its conviction of the importance of simplicty. When as a schoolboy he was required to memorize Goldsmith's "Traveller," he tied his book to the handles of his plough, and learned the poem as he made his contribution to the support of the school. There was a tradition that he and his schoolmates long preceded Emerson in breakfasting on apple pie, for which incidentally they had gathered and peeled the apples, and ploughed and helped to harvest the wheat. The serious and practical discipline of this honored school, inculcating by word and deed frugality and rectitude, contributed undoubtedly to that boy's sternly upright character under the strains of later life.

At the outbreak of the Civil War, Isaac Pugh had become senior partner of a prosperous and enterprising firm manufacturing wallpaper. They had large contracts with southern dealers. When the war brought bankruptcy to southern cities these contracts became valueless. As the eldest and most experienced of the three partners, Grandfather Pugh felt responsible, and refused to avail himself of the bankruptcy law. He shouldered the debts of the firm, sacrificed almost all his property and helped unweariedly by our Grandmother, struggled and saved throughout fifteen years of continuous effort and succeeded, on the salary of a modest position in the Philadelphia post office, in paying principal and interest, before blindness made work impossible at the age of eighty-three.

Sarah Pugh, Grandfather's sister, born in 1800, and thus a year his junior, small and slight of figure while he was tall and gaunt, silent almost as himself, was an eager Abolitionist. If she had had her way, their ivy-clad, conventional-looking old home for fifty years would have been a station of the Underground Railroad, harboring from time to time fugitive slaves on their way to Canada and freedom. Long after the Civil War, she was still gently grieved that the home of her deeply beloved brother had had no share in that secret, dangerous protest.

Naturally, I remember only conversations after Mr. Lincoln's death, when his Proclamation of Emancipation had long put an end to that strange, systematic violation of the law, so successfully carried out by the most conscientious citizens conceivable!

To every suggestion of this lost opportunity, however, our grandfather replied, throughout his long life:

"The Civil War was fought to save the Union, and to prevent the extension of slavery to the free States. These ends were achieved without the use of this house."

Following this came quite regularly our grandmother's quiet comment:

"I have never been clear that it was not possible for this country to do as England did—buy the slaves and set them free without a war."

There was never any further conversation; each had borne testimony after the manner of the Society of Friends. Our gentle Grandmother's rule of action was: Nothing in life is so important as peace, especially peace in the home.

Not until I had gone to college and come back to this harmonious trio, did the significance of the fact dawn upon my mind that Greataunt Sarah, after teaching school a quarter century, had retired at the age of fifty years from her profession, to give her time entirely to promoting the antislavery movement, peace, woman suffrage, the single standard of morals for men and women, and free trade.

Stenography was then unknown to women, if indeed stenography had become known beyond the bounds of Washington, D.C., where few Congressmen had secretaries competent to use it. All her work was done through letters in writing as clear as print. Scores of times have I heard her murmur to long-staying ladies calling upon our grandmother: "I am glad to have seen Thee; and now I have a little writing to do."

No physician performing operations at fixed times in a hospital and keeping office hours day by day; no lawyer moving from office to court-room and back again; no teacher in school, was ever more methodically active than the silent little Quakeress who sat at least half of every day at her desk, in her room, writing letters to Cobden and Bright, to John Stuart Mill, Lady Stanley of Alderley and the Dutchess of Sutherland, and later on for many years, to Mrs. Josephine Butler, of sainted memory, throughout her terribly painful crusade to abolish the Contagious Diseases Acts in England.

A whole new world opened to me the day when I first observed that she never under any circumstances used sugar, even in tea. In Philadelphia Friends' parlance I asked:

"Aunt Sarah, why does Thee never eat sugar? and why are Thy underclothes linen even in winter?" I had seen her skilfully mending the fine linen while she talked to me about her English correspondents.

"Cotton was grown by slaves, and sugar also," she replied, "so I decided many years ago never to use either, and to bring these facts to the attention of my friends."

Not meaning to be impertinent, I said: "Aunt Sarah, does Thee really think any slaves were Freed because thee did not use sugar or cotton?"

Perfectly tranquil was her reply: "Dear child, I can never know that any slave was personally helped; but I had to live with my own conscience."

A dear and honored friend of the household in Germantown was Lucretia Mott, the internationally beloved preacher of the Society of Friends, who lived within easy driving distance and came occasionally on Sunday afternoon. In winter these two frail little figures sometimes sat in the charming back parlor of the old house before a cheerful log fire knitting in protest against the prevailing rigid Sabbatarianism of Philadelphia. This must have been solely to appease their own consciences, for I cannot remember any other visitor arriving while they were thus occupied. Nothing in our grandmother's demeanor ever expressed the trial that she endured when these mild, protesting citizens carried on their Sunday afternoon knitting on the porch, in the long spring, summer and autumn of the mild Philadelphia climate, visible to passersby who might be shocked, but could never be enlightened by their procedure which they had no means of interpreting. Lucretia Mott's great-granddaughter, Marianna Parrish, is my sister-in-law, wife of my brother, Albert Bartram Kelley.

Under Aunt Sarah's exceedingly fine, close-fitting cap of almost transparent net, her silver hair was bobbed in all my memories of her. This was the nearest approach possible for her to freedom in dress. She had not, like Grandfather Pugh, married "out of meeting." She remained true to the rigidly simple garb of the Friends as long as she lived. But so far as I know, she was unique in her half-century long silent protest against the compulsory usage of long hair for women.

From this grandaunt, Fathers' conviction that children must know the life of boys and girls less fortunate than themselves received strong confirmation, and was broadened to early concern for the lot of all women. To me she seemed conscience incarnate, and it was quite natural that, as a girl of fifteen years, I received from Aunt Sarah reprints of Mrs. Josephine Butler's addresses to the Queen, and to Parliament, for immediate abolition of segregation of women in lock hospitals in England and India. In the vain effort to protect the health of the British army, these concealed, secreted troops of unfortunate women were permanently maintained out of English taxes.

The injustice, the suffering, the inevitably unsuccessful attempt in another country to reduce loathsome disease by oppressing women, haunted the conscience of this Pennsylvania Friend as though these evils had been present in Philadelphia where she lived. And like Father, she followed the principle that no deeply rooted evil can ever be finally eradicated except by stirring the minds of the on-coming generation to abiding awareness of the changes that they will have to complete.

Aunt Sarah never wrote for publications or spoke in meetings, and her money contributions from her salary as a teacher, from which she conscientiously saved for her old age (she died at eighty-three) must have been most modest. Her influence both within and without the Society of Friends was exerted largely through personal friendships which she cultivated assiduously.

In our era of amplifiers, radio inserts in moving-picture shows, full-page advertisements in metropolitan dailies, and all the troop of libelers and vilifiers, spreading their perversions over a continent, it is hard, indeed, to recreate in imagination the faith and patience of reformers using such quiet methods in the first three-quarters of the nineteenth century. Yet it is a matter of history that, in 131 years, the protests of Pennsylvania Friends never ceased —between 1732 when Friends in Rittenhouse Meeting adopted a minute that "It is the sense of this meeting that it is unseemly for Friends to hold human beings, as chattels," and forthwith set free all their own slaves—and 1863, when President Lincoln issued the Proclamation of Emancipation. And their methods, which never provoked opposition or resistance, were far more effectual than appeared upon the surface.

Our mother's own father, Henry L. Bonsall, married "out of meeting" and we, his grandchildren, were therefore never "birthright" Quakers. Our mother's father by adoption, Isaac Pugh, having married into the Unitarian family of Kay, close and intimate friends of Dr. Priestly, was also "out of meeting." It is characteristic of Friend Isaac Pugh that he gave our mother, in 1839, a piano as a birthday present and thereafter, having thus again disregarded the tenets of the Society of Friends, continued to sit throughout the Sunday meeting on the last seat at the rear of the meeting-house, except when he accompanied our grandmother to the Unitarian Church whose minister was Samuel Longfellow, brother of the poet, succeeded for several years by Mr. Charles Gordon Ames.

In this atmosphere of peace, affection, obedience to conscience, and faithful adherence to conviction, our mother grew up, and it was in this Quaker home in Germantown that I spent most of the happiest days of my childhood.

Partly because of my mother's fear of the possible loss of her last surviving daughter, and no less because of my unusual susceptibility to infection, my school life was almost nil. I could never attend regularly or complete a school year; my longest uninterrupted attendance being five or six months beginning with my thirteenth birthday, at Miss Marianna Longstreth's school for girls in Philadelphia. A few weeks in a delightful little school in Germantown when I was eight years old had ended in bed and a winter of rheumatism. Attendance in 1868 at the Friends' School at Fifteenth and Race Streets, Philadelphia, was cut short by scarlet fever, due doubtless to travel in the filthy horse-cars.

Fortunately this disaster did not occur until I had garnered several precious memories. Never to be forgotten are the Fourth Day meetings in the austere simplicity and peaceful quiet of Friends' meeting-house, boys sitting on one side, girls on the other, and Friends facing the school, awaiting in reverent silence the possible moving of the Spirit, to bear testimony to the Truth in the presence of the young. The benches were of wood, uncushioned; the weekly hour seemed endless and was brightened only by the flickering hope that the Spirit might begin promptly, so that belated admonitions could not interfere with the outdoor play hour that followed the service.

Someone had given me, as a philopena gift, an almost invisible tiny diamond in a thin thread of a gold ring. In order that my nine years-old thoughts should not be distracted, this was left every Fourth Day (Wednesday morning with a teacher who stood at our entrance. It was duly returned to me at the close of the session.

An interesting item of the Friends' School life was the pupils' share in continuous help to the school for the children of Freedmen (former slaves emancipated in 1863). This school was maintained by two women on St. Helena island off the coast of South Carolina.* There were frequent requests from our teachers for garments and books that *we liked* ourselves. It was carefully explained that while gifts might be sent that were outgrown, there was never any sending of things that were out-worn or cast off. This practical sharing in the early effort to educate the Negroes has led many boys and girls to keep on helping throughout life. To it, in part, I trace my active participation during the past sixteen years in the work of the National Association for the Advancement of Colored People

A painful incident of this brief school attendance was passing a large, forbidding-looking brick building and seeing from the car window on our homeward way, when we had half-day sessions ending at noon, little skinny girls waiting on the sidewalk before the

---

* Penn School, the oldest school for Negroes in the South, founded by Dr. Towne of Philadelphia, and her associate, Miss Murray. The work is carried forward today by their successors, Rossa B. Cooley and Grace Bigelow House; and readers of *The Survey* will recall Miss Cooley's series of articles in 1923-24 in the *Survey Graphic*, to be brought out this fall as a New Republic book: *Home of the Freed*.

closed doors. The building was a textile mill, and the children were "hands" returning from their noon half-hour for dinner.

At that time children, even in Massachusetts, could work ten hours a day in a cotton mill, at the age of ten years; and Pennsylvania had no limit upon ages or hours of work by day or by night.

In 1871 the family were spending the autumn in the Alleghenies to give our mother a change of scene after the latest, dreadful bereavement. We were within easy reach of the Pennsylvania railroad station at Altoona, and of several steel towns. Our father used the opportunity to show me a spectacle which had the interest and charm of novelty—the manufacture of steel by the newly introduced Bessemer process. It was, indeed, a terrifying sight. An enormous pearshaped vessel filled with iron ore was heated many hours and then, at a signal, all people except the minimum number of employees responsible for the dangerous manipulation, were ordered to the outside edge of the circular building. At a second signal, the monster vessel was inverted and the molten metal, white-hot and fluid, was turned into molds of sand waiting for it on the earthen floor of the building. These molds were of the same size throughout the industry, and were known throughout the English-speaking world as "pigs." This branch of manufacture was known as the pig-iron industry, although the technical name of each piece of iron at the completion of the process was *ingot*.

No weirder scene could be conceived than the general dark interior and the locally blinding glare of the furnace that supplied heat for melting the iron ore. Then the moment of frightful suspense, when, if anything had gone wrong, several lives must inevitably have been lost. That has occurred more than once in the long course of development of the Bessemer method of transforming iron ore into steel; and still occurs from time to time under the newer methods.

WILLIAM DARRAH KELLEY

FLORENCE KELLEY AS A STUDENT AT CORNELL

When Coeducation
Was Young

Entering college was for me an almost sacramental experience.
Two long years I had lived for it, since that lonely morning
when I found, in the otherwise empty waste-basket in my father's
study, Cornell's offer of equal intellectual opportunity to women.
Cornell was the first eastern university to make this glorious offer.
The ideal of Ezra Cornell far exceeded everything that had gone
before. He said in varying forms, on different occasions: "I would
found an institution where anyone may study any subject!" This I
read in the fourth annual report and forthwith begged Father to let
me prepare. Not until then did I know that, years before, he had
worked with Andrew D. White to get the Morrill Act adopted by
Congress, under which land-grant colleges and universities now
exist. Mr. White became the first President of Cornell, but was
much absent, while I was a student, as Ambassador to Berlin.

Careful enquiry soon revealed that there was no school in
Philadelphia equipped to fit a girl thoroughly for college, low as
the standard of entrance requirements then was. It was my gro-
tesque experience to be prepared by tutors and governesses
themselves not college-bred. My college preparation was in fact
pure sham. Only an excellent verbal memory which enabled me to

cram, coupled with the lax college standards, permitted me to enter
the freshman class in 1876, with all the entrance conditions inevitable for a girl from a great city which afforded not one fitting
school for girls.

I was then sixteen. I entered Cornell just as the first women
graduated from that University, and in the ensuing decade I was to
share the liberty and equality that characterized the early days of
co-education; was to be denied opportunity for graduate work in
the University of Pennsylvania in my own city of Philadelphia,
only to be admitted less than a year later to the Law School of
Zurich, a university in that land of freedom which had, for a
generation, opened wide its doors to men and women from all the
world on equal terms.

The dissolving concepts in men's minds—the expanding opportunities for women in intellectual life, in politics, in industry, the
gains and setbacks of sixty years do not stand out like blues and
reds on a wall map; but it is easy to gauge progress in social institutions and thought by selecting an outstanding event, and marking
changes among familiar things.

Such an event for me, in the summer before going to Cornell in
September 1876, was the Centennial Exposition in Philadelphia. I
see again the first day, with President Grant leading the procession
to the place of the opening ceremonies. The crowd was terrific as
crowds went in those days, and the Exposition, the first international one in the country, seemed overwhelmingly impressive to
my young eyes. Many foreign exhibits would have been beautiful in
any surrounding, among them the porcelains and pottery wares
from England, France and Belgium.

The thrill of the summer was going into a booth in the Fair
grounds at a time agreed upon with some friend in another booth,
and conversing over the telephone. That was the miracle of that
Exposition. It was perhaps, the next great technical step toward
unifying the world since the laying of the Atlantic cable. In memory
I link it with an episode three years later in France, that stands out
as vividly.

Among Father's most valued correspondents was Monsieur
Henri Cernuschi, an Italian who had been an active patriot when
Italy was becoming united, and before the first Victor Emmanuel
became King. M. Cernuschi, by conviction an anti-monarchist
Republican, then became a citizen of Paris in protest against the

lost opportunity of United Italy to become a republic. He invited us to breakfast at his museum in the Parc Monceau, a superb building filled with rare oriental bronzes, which M. Cernuschi occupied throughout the remainder of his life, and bequeathed with his entire fortune to the City of Paris. He was the most beautiful old man I have ever seen, with large deep-set hazel eyes, snowy hair, and black brows. His imposing surroundings, which would have made a less impressive person shrink to insignificance, seemed a harmonious and suitable setting for this noble figure. His was the first house in Paris lighted by electricity, and he told us with keen amusement how he had arranged a great ball, when his treasures were all assembled ready to be viewed. Unhappily the ladies arrived with faces arranged for candlelight. At first glimpse of the utterly unmodulated crude electric light they fled, and the ball became "what you call in English a stag party. That was a sad anti-climax!"

Today we take the telephone and the electric bulb for granted without enquiring how many of our current ideas, social, educational and political antedate them.

Far less conspicuous, though perhaps as significant was another change in our habits foreshadowed at the Centennial. A lasting gift of Europe to America was in the field of foods, made by an enterprising Austrian, who had already acquainted Vienna with a cream of tomato soup, and who introduced his bakeries and restaurants into this country largely by means of this delightful viand, since appropriated everywhere. Indeed our interest in diversifying food products and improving the diet of people of all origins and traditions has never since diminished in peace or war time.

How few of us realize that the entry of women's clubs as a permanent element in American life was contemporaneous with the coming of tomato soup! And with what fear and trembling one of the earliest clubs was founded, and our brother man's approval openly sought by the world-old way of the stomach. An example of the continued interest aroused by the Exposition was the procedure of the New Century (women's) Club of Philadelphia, founded in that year. The charter members included several suffragists, a journalist or two, a few teachers and some philanthropists, the instigator of the adventure being Mrs. Eliza Turner, writer of some charmingly humorous, and a few beautiful poems. This group, eager to avoid ridicule by the press, and to gain friends among conservative men, made its first public appearance in a fine old house of the Girard estate. To a few carefully chosen guests it gave a Nine Cent Dinner, and made known its intention of establishing a cooking school. The dinner was superlatively successful; the costs were convincingly set forth; the food was tempting and sustaining; and the speaking was long remembered as full of wit and savor. The success of the club was assured from that evening.

Looking back a half century, however, it is hard to believe that all those precautions were necessary for inaugurating one of the conservatively useful movements of women in these United States.

I was free to pass every alternate day at the Fair. The other day was spent struggling with conditions left over from my June college examinations in Greek, Latin and algebra. In the educational department I saw more than once an impressive figure studying the exhibits of the Massachusetts Institute of Technology and other kindred schools. Unaccompanied by a secretary, this gentleman worked all the morning with notebooks and enquiries addressed to the head of the educational exhibit. Quite unaware of the annoyance that I might be causing the distinguished stranger, I also spent mornings in the division of Education. What held him longest was the beautiful contribution of the Russian Imperial Technical Schools. Before the end of the summer I learned that this student was Dom Pedro, then still Emperor of Brazil.

Occasionally I persuaded some young friend to go with me, but rarely more than once. I was slow, too interested in the things which might be useful to Father, who was too absorbed in the excitements of the campaign preceding the Hayes-Tilden presidential election, to spend strength in visiting the Exposition. It might well have broken his heart, for the general bad taste and bad quality of our own products has never been approached at any later World's Fair. Only the "infancy" of our industries palliated our impudence in inviting the world to look at them, and send goods for comparison with them. There is, however, some slight solace in the memory of a candid Englishman's famous reference to their exhibits in 1851 as "cheap and nasty."

The change, seen from this distance, between the Centennial in 1876 and the Columbian Exposition in Chicago in 1893, less than twenty years later, was indeed marvelous. The dominant note in 1893 was beauty in architecture, in lighting, in grouping of buildings and exhibits, and finally in the exhibits themselves. The

Chicago Fair registered the coming of age of American industry and engineering on its technical side.

My freshman year was one continued joy. An-hungered and athirst for learning, and for young companionship, which now abounded on every side, and aware in every waking hour of the surrounding outdoor beauty, here was indeed delight. Little did we care that there was no music, no theater, almost no library; that the stairs to the lecture halls were wooden, and the classrooms heated with coal stoves. No one, so far as I know, read a daily paper, or subscribed for a monthly or a quarterly. Our current gossip was Froude's life of Carlyle. We read only bound volumes. I do not believe that the New York *Nation* had one subscriber in Ithaca. That was the year when President Hayes was "counted in" by a Congressional commission sitting in New Orleans. Father was sent thither as an observer and wrote me about the exciting occasion. But none of my friends among the students was interested enough to listen to his letters. The one person outside our own group of whom we heard with alert interest was Dr. Mary Putnam Jacobi, the first woman graduate from the Paris School of Medicine who had recently begun to practice in New York City. I was deeply impressed when Ruth Putnam, her sister a junior, brought me an invitation to join a group reading Swinburne with Miss M. Carey Thomas, then a senior. But if there was sustained, serious reading, thought or discussion occurring on the campus, outside of the science laboratories, I was not aware of it. The next year, however, I shared in founding the first Cornell Social Science Club, and served as its first secretary.

The elective system carried to the utmost extreme tempted my inexperience. Undismayed by entrance conditions in Latin, Greek and mathematics, I embarked upon a schedule of twenty-five hours a week of ancient and modern languages and mathematics, besides those heavy arrears. Yet I always had two hours daily for outdoor exercise. I listened and recited, studied, memorized, acquired. I walked, rode, drove and danced.

The few modest grey stone or brick buildings on the campus formed an unobtrusive part of a gloriously beautiful region. They crowded the eastern hillside, above a lovely valley, with Lake Cayuga stretching northward. In the early evening a long, slowly changing pageant filled with gold and color the great bowl of the southern end of the valley, brimming with the green of treetops under radiant cloud masses. In the brilliant sunshine of late September, cloud shadows moved all day long across the western hillside aflame with blazing autumn leaves.

Bayard Taylor, the Pennsylvania poet, visiting Cornell as a non-resident lecturer, on his return from Europe, assured us that the natural beauty of our campus excelled any that he had seen abroad.

Bryn Mawr, then recently founded, and Princeton, have led towards a future with the charm of unity, of harmony and dignity in university architecture, though the natural gifts of their sites were in no way comparable to the loveliness of Ithaca's eastern hill with its gorges and streams, its northward lake, and its ever-moving picture of clouds above the curves of the western and southern hill. It was a marvelous appeal through every hour of every day that greeted those early students.

Happy indeed were we that our student life ended before the days of hugeness, of mass-production of learning. Little did we foresee what the Philistines could achieve in a half century. Without previous general plan, without appeal to the imagination, every variety of modern academic architecture, except the Pittsburgh skyscraper, encumbers that once beautiful hilltop. And now there is a drive for a Gothic edifice! To see from the campus in broad sweep the western glory of the late afternoon that was the joy of our youth, students now must climb, like tourists, flights of stairs inside tall buildings, and gaze through windows or mount in aeroplanes.

Cornell under the Morrill Act was among the early land-grant universities. It was created by the generous response of Congress to Ezra Cornell's noble offer to carry the early costs, thus saving New York's allotment of forest land from loss such as state universities had suffered where no benefactor made possible the holding of a forest gift while its value appreciated.

A foremost plan of Mr. Cornell, who had been a wage-earner in early boyhood and longed to use his wealth to make learning accessible to other youth, was to attract young laborers who could work their way through college. We all knew this and revered his memory.

The vast development of schools of agriculture, engineering, law, medicine and science, the superb library, and the excellent position of the department of household science—these embodiments of his ideal must have rejoiced the heart of Ezra Cornell could he have lived to see them. Though boys and girls of limited means find putting themselves through by hard labor no more feasible at Cornell than elsewhere, generous gifts in scholarships of the state and the cities of New York, go far to fulfil Mr. Cornell's aspiration for opportunity for all.

Those were spacious days at Cornell. We were utterly unconscious of the freedom of body, mind and estate of faculty and students that prevailed throughout the young university. We were as unaware of that freedom as of the presence of the surrounding atmosphere, it was so absolutely taken for granted.

It was in 1876 that President White published his *Warfare of Science*, a prelude to his copious work, *History of the Warfare of Science with Theology in Christendom*, published in 1906.

Goldwin Smith who was, after many years as Regius Professor of history at Oxford, considering coming to America, had been brought to Cornell as a regular lecturer from 1869 to 1871, and came thereafter at intervals from Canada, for courses of lectures from the point of view of English Liberalism. There were frequent campus references to his statement that he was "used to a university with roots in the past, but Cornell's roots in the future appeared prodigious." In his reminiscences published more than thirty years later he comments upon the fact that Ithaca, even after it became a rapidly-growing little city, needed for years only a single elderly constable, so thoroughly self-governing and law-abiding were the students.

Compulsory chapel was as far from our horizon as compulsory military drill. Students who elected drill received it in the men's gymnasium. Co-education being then largely experimental (established so far as I know, only at Oberlin, Antioch, Swarthmore and Earlham, and at the few then-existing state universities) acted selectively upon women candidates for admission to Cornell. We were a serious, self-conscious body of pioneers, in no need of student government or any other.

About seventy girls were lodged in Sage College, the first dormitory, generously designed for a far larger number. But no one was required to live in the dormitory. Such a requirement would, in those days of liberty and equality, have met vigorous protest. Rather the authorities encouraged us to share our half-empty dining room with men students, whom we were free to invite, six men and six girls to each table. An invitation was for the student's college course, and the company varied, as seniors went out and freshmen came in. Of this company were M. Carey Thomas, Ruth Putnam, a daughter of the founder of the Putnam publishing house and author of a biography of William the Silent; Charles W. Ames, afterwards head of a St. Paul law publishing company; Karl Volkmann, head of the Volkmann School; Archer Randolph; Margaret Hicks, to whom there will be future references; James A. Haight, an active member of the Seattle Port Authority; and Harriet May Mills, long a leading suffragist, now a member of the New York State Hospital Commission.

From this companionship developed marriages and life-long friendships. A generation later there were at Harvard a son of Charles W. Ames, a son of Karl Volkmann, a son of Archer Randolph, and two of my own. Several friendships have been cherished throughout life and continue in the next generation; and the prospect is that, beginning next fall, the first of the grandchildren may enter college a leader of the third generation of that group.

Two members of that cheerful table company, Archer Randolph and Margaret Hicks, died sadly early.

There were no extra-curricular activities for girls, no athletics, not even basketball. Our Sage College gymnasium bare of equipment stood permanently empty except for a piano daily used by our table company for dancing after dinner and supper, and this was a symbol. Here and there upon the horizon some lone woman physician stood ready for patients; Dr. Hannah Longshore had been our family doctor from my childhood. But the epoch of outdoor life even for a generation enterprising enough to break down barriers against indoor study had not yet dawned. The health movevent for women students began with the appointment of physicians in girls' colleges and physical examinations for entrants, with records of weights and measurements. The concept of health for all and play for all was not yet implanted in the American mind. Universities were for minds, not bodies; they had been throughout the ages the domain of men. Women's ancient concern for nurture, growth, and the storing up of vigor was still limited to the home. The nursing profession as entitled to rank with medicine in the structure of universities was beyond the range of dreams. No estimate can ever be made of the precious lives of gifted youth that perished during hundreds of years of control by men alone.

Cornell men students had already a name for intercollegiate races, and David Starr Jordan was then better known as coach of the successful Cornell crew than as an exponent of the theory of evolution, a leader for peace and authority on the anatomy of fishes.

After the westward pilgrimage when, at twelve years old, I learned on the plains of Wyoming to ride a thoroughly well-broken mustang, I had never been without a saddle horse. I now possessed a broad, low, uncovered vehicle known as a phaeton, which we used all day long on Saturdays, a group of friends, men and girls, after early breakfast tramping five or six miles to a cider mill, or a gorge and waterfall, carrying in the phaeton lunch for all. Two or three rode together a mile or two, to a country road, then tied the horse to a fence and walked forward, the next comers taking their turn, until the last laggards arrived at the common meeting-ground. It was characteristic of the region that neither luncheon nor vehicle was ever interfered with. There were no lectures or recitations on Saturday, and nothing was farther from our minds than squandering a radiant autumn holiday in collateral reading.

After a gay and delightful Christmas holiday, our home being the center of a group of Cornell students, I went back to college in 1879 carrying, unhappily, a diptheria infection and arrived in Ithaca in a stupor. The students who, unaware of this, had kindly come in an open sleigh to meet me, found me unconscious. On the way to Sage College we passed the home of Dr. Winslow who joined us. He spent the rest of the night vainly seeking an "experienced nurse" with students as messengers, and of course without a telephone.

Although Ithaca had been ten years a university town, in 1879 an infirmary was not yet thought of, and hospital nurses were not to be found outside of New York City. Because the untrained local nurse was ignorant of the danger of overdosing and forgot the doctor's order to discontinue after ten days, I received large doses of brandy at two hours' intervals, from January to mid-May, following strychina, and other poisons. Three years out of college were the penalty paid for that illness and that untrained nurse.

Not until March 1882 could I return to Ithaca, when my thesis, with examinations in a multitude of subjects brought me a bachelor's degree and, two years later, when the Cornell Chapter of Phi Beta Kappa was formed, a key as well.

Immediately after receiving my degree at Cornell, I applied to the University of Pennsylvania for permission to enter for further study in advanced Greek. After long failure of the faculty to respond, Father addressed to the trustees a formal request for my admission. The reply of Dr. Horace Howard Furness, editor of the Variorum edition of Shakespeare and son of Dr. William H. Furness, Father's friend of many years, was perhaps not surprising for those days. The ground of Dr. Furness' opposition to my entrance was that, the older he grew and the more he knew people, the lower his opinion of them became and the more abhorrent the thought of young men and women meeting in the classroom.

Not for several years did we know the real reason of the refusal of the trustees. In 1882, Professor Francis Jackson, a distant relative of my grandfather, Isaac Pugh, was dean of the classical department and debarred thereby from comment upon the decision. Only after he had severed connection with the university could he write me, explaining that I was not admitted because in 1882 there was no advanced Greek at the university!

It is a far cry from that refusal to the granting by the University of Pennsylvania, a few years ago, of a Ph.D. degree to a young colored woman, bachelors' and doctors' degrees being long since common for white women.

My intent was to study law and this setback did not lead me to abandon it. Graduate Greek had meant only a vestibule to a law school, and the path thither now developed naturally through acquaintances formed around our table at Sage College. My brother William and I sailed in December 1882 for the Riviera via Liverpool, London and Paris. His temporary blindness detained us until spring at Avignon, and fortunately never recurred. This was a lonely sojourn because few people in the little Provencale city spoke French. One brilliant evening, however, stands out in the midst of that grim, gray experience. Miss Thomas stopped over-night at our hotel on her way to Italy. She had been studying at Leipzig and had just received at Zurich her doctor's degree *summa cum laude*, and was a most cheerful and stimulating companion, the more so by contrast with our long loneliness. She returned to America and became first dean, then president, of Bryn Mawr. Our chance meeting suggested Zurich for me as a last resort, if Oxford should prove impossible; and to Zurich I went. At that point, however, our ways parted, although to this day the uncompleted task of breaking barriers to the full intellectual life shares with the social claims of industry my permanent incandescent interest.

The century-long struggle to open wide the new world of higher education was hardly more than begun in my girlhood. It is by no means over yet, while the law schools of Harvard and Columbia still exclude women, and Negro students strive now as we strove then for admission on equal terms everywhere.

So long as women hardly exist as full professors in state universities, and Dr. Alice Hamilton's experience as a member of the medical faculty of Harvard remains unique, that struggle is far from ended. Equal opportunity in the field of education does not mean remaining forever students, it means also teaching in the highest ranks, and sharing work and responsibility of administration. It is a noble distinction of the University of Chicago, well worthy of special notice, that Sophonisba Breckenridge and Edith Abbott are full professors, and Miss Abbott is dean of the *Graduate* School of Social Service Administration.

The dearth of women trustees and regents indicates how little the great national organizations of women have appreciated their own power, and the vast amount of hard work that remains to be done. If, as these enormous bodies grew in influence, we had appreciated the efficacy of insistent criticism and unwearied persuasion, women trustees and regents of state, county and city institutions of learning would now be everywhere at work. They could have made impossible the policy of limiting undergraduates women in co-educational universities to daughters living at home or students in dormitories. This is an odious barrier.

Women in large numbers on administrative boards could have increased vastly the paltry number of internships open to women; for they could have stood for the principle that hospitals (state, city or county) can not, if maintained out of taxes, discriminate on grounds of sex against candidates offering equally good credentials.

Endowed hospitals, also, could have been made aware that remaining tax-exempt may depend upon giving women a fair share of internships.

A stimulus which we have failed generally to apply is withholding gifts and bequests from schools which discriminate against women. These are ungracious measures, but they are obviously necessary. I remember how Miss Garrett of Baltimore opened, long ago, the

Johns Hopkins Medical School, which celebrated in 1926 its semi-centennial. She agreed to a large gift, and withheld it until women students were granted equal opportunities. The school has both admitted women, and had on its medical faculty a woman of distinction. Yet Dr. Florence Sabin, with title and duties of professor of histology, never exercised the administrative functions of a full professor. Now her position with the Rockefeller Foundation is equivalent to a full professorship.

It is startling that Johns Hopkins, founded to be a pioneer, lists today not one woman as *full* professor. Great is the social injury following the grudging treatment of women who desire to enter the medical profession.

Astonishing too is the limited number of women full professors in co-educational colleges and professional schools. In state universities the few who have the title and work of *full* professor are often hampered by lower salaries and scant appropriation for equipment. Among distinguished names are Anna Botsford Comstock at Cornell, Louise Pound at Nebraska, Jessica Peixotto at California, Dr. Eliza Mosher at Michigan, who as professor of hygiene and dean of women in 1886, was the first full professor but not in the Medical School. Barbara Bartlett of the Department of Hygiene and Public Health is a full professor and a member of the faculty of the Medical Department.

In Household Economics, their own great contribution to university work, women are of course to be found in considerable numbers as full professors.

It is amazing that Wellesley and Lake Erie alone, apparently among women's colleges enjoying the prestige of a half century as independent degree-conferring foundations, have always had women at the head, Vassar and Smith having always had men as presidents. Miss Thomas' long service as President at Bryn Mawr was preceded by that of a man.

On every hand laments resound because of the dearth of men equipped to meet the demand of unparalleled throngs of candidates for admission. How greatly enriched the students of today would be, if the women of ability and academic training, who have during the past half-century been discouraged from fitting themselves for posts of the greatest responsibility, had been generously welcomed and encouraged!

Behold a shining example of this crabbed spirit in college life.

Margaret Hicks, a fellow student only a year my senior, took charge of me that snowy night in January, when I so nearly died at Cornell, risking her life, for anti-toxin did not then exist. She was the beloved friend of my youth, and there followed a friendship between her mother and myself precious still when Mrs. Louis Prang is celebrating her ninetieth birthday, a beautiful, dignified and gracious woman.

When I received my degree, Margaret and I helped to found a New England branch of the Association of Collegiate Alumnae. After her early death in 1883, her mother wished to aid in work which had so keenly interested her only child, and applied for membership in the Assocation, but was ineligible, not being herself an alumna. She cherished, however, throughout twenty-two years of work with the Prang Educational Company, the desire to become a member.

Mrs. Prang finally entered Radcliffe, following a course of study there with the Harvard Lowell lectures, and received from Harvard University in June 1916, in the eightieth year, the certificate issued to men and women alike with the title Associate in Arts. The Association of Collegiate Alumnae which Mrs. Prang then joined has since become the American Association of University Women.

Harvard University offered in 1917 graduate courses to which women were admitted. Mrs. Prang entered the Graduate School of Education and received in June 1921, in the eighty-fifth year, the degree of Master of Education of Harvard University.

Thereupon a young Harvard professor, deploring the admission of women to the School of Education, said: "Yes, women are coming in. They can't be kept out. And when they are everywhere in the University it will be recognized that Mrs. Prang was the camel's nose. However," he added after a pause, "the College will never grant a degree to a woman."

In my own profession, the exclusion of women from the best equipped law schools with greatest prestige is most injurious for it delays the needed membership in the courts of women with every requisite qualification. The Supreme Court of the United States has taught us, in recent years that, until this change is made, the most defenseless of our people, women and children who must earn their living in industry, need not hope for social justice.

JANE ADDAMS IN 1889

JULIA LATHROP

FLORENCE KELLEY AND HER HUSBAND,
LAZARE WISCHNEWETZKY, WITH THEIR SON, NICHOLAS,
AND LAZARE'S MOTHER, 1885

My Novitiate

My father's daughter could never from early childhood be long unaware of the developing struggle for women's political rights. A welcome incident in our London sojourn in the summer of 1883, when the family were in England with Father convalescent, was a call from Susan B. Anthony. From the beginning, at Seneca Falls in 1848, of the movement for women's suffrage, Father and Grandaunt Sarah were permanently interested. He was an early and frequent speaker for both abolition and suffrage, and after Representative Sargent of California went to the Senate, Father became sponsor for the suffrage Amendment in the House. He deplored every break, by reason of difference of opinion among suffragists as to state or federal procedure, in the long struggle which he would gladly have seen a continuous campaign for immediate submission by Congress.

When Miss Anthony succeeded in having a suffrage convention held in Washington during every Congress, she relied upon Father as a regular speaker. Out of this usage grew a friendship which lasted throughout his life. Showing the sincerity of both, I remember one characteristic incident. When Father became chairman of the Committee on Ways and Means, he pledged himself to meet with the subcommittees, not merely to preside at formal meetings of the whole. Miss Anthony had advertised him for a certain evening as a speaker at the Suffrage Convention. Unhappily there was also a subcommittee meeting that evening of the Committee on Ways and Means to consider the general subject of acids. I attended Miss Anthony's convention, and my anxiety was second only to her own as speaker after speaker was introduced and Father failed to appear. As the evening closed Miss Anthony said: "This is a new and painful illustration of the lack of respect for the vote even among men who are convinced advocates of suffrage. Even Judge Kelley considers the tariff on vinegar of greater importance than votes."

I went home with my heart in my shoes. I foresaw Father's indignation that, after a quarter century's active allegiance to a cause still sufficiently unpopular, he was ridiculed by the great leader whom he counted a friend. At breakfast next morning I watched anxiously as he opened the paper. I had not courage to open it myself. Great was my bewilderment and relief to hear him laugh and say:"The good old Major! I'm afraid I deserved that."

Learning of his very serious illness, Miss Anthony came to call in London. I see them now—he was lying on a couch, exhausted and wan, and Miss Anthony, wearing her famous paisley shawl, sitting straight as a young birch tree, suggesting by her posture his affectionate nickname of the Major. In the presence of what was to prove, seven years later, after a gallant struggle, his fatal illness, there was that day no merriment in either face. And how far they were from believing that the coming of suffrage in the United States was still thirty-seven years in the future!

In the decade 1876 to 1886, I shared in the new university life open to women here and in Switzerland. As frequent companion of my father, a Republican member of Congress from Pennsylvania, I was already conscious of tremendous initiatives in the swift development of American industry. Amid endless talk of iron and steel and tariffs, I cherished his charge that it was for his generation to create the great industry and for ours to devise methods of just distribution of its products. I was to offer a slender study of The Law and the Child for my Cornell bachelor's degree, one among the first theses on such an economic subject offered in those days by an American senior; to start three months after graduating, an evening school for working girls in Philadelphia which still survives under the name the New Century Guild; and to have my childhood impressions of American glass-house boys and textile mill-girls deepened by a visit to the English Black Country. And following my reverent listening to the debates of my elders, American protectionists and English free traders, I was to come in contact in the halls of a Swiss university with ardent students from a dozen countries who had been caught by the new wildfire of Socialism, then spreading over the whole Continent.

Even in the United States (despite the classical preoccupation of the colleges) the period was not without its ferment of ideals and compunctions destined later to issue in various creative movements. Julia Lathrop was at Vassar, Jane Addams was reading the Greek Testament with a beloved teacher on Sundays beside her daily work at Rockford Seminary, which did not become a college until she was a member of the Board of Trustees. Carrie Chapman Catt was a student at Iowa State College, and Anna Howard Shaw, having studied at Albion, Michigan, was taking graduate courses in medicine and theology at Boston University.

My Cornell thesis on The Law and the Child* compared with the scholarly documents so common today, had been slight enough. For me it was of incalculable importance. The choice of the subject followed naturally upon Father's years of effort to enlist me permanently in behalf of less fortunate children. The thesis itself completely accomplished that purpose. The winter of 1881-82, when I was still, as a convalescent, absent from Cornell, I spent with Father in the mild climate of Washington, working upon it. There I found in the Library of Congress all the authorities on the common and statutory law affecting children; and quite as much to my purpose, the official reports of the few state bureaus of labor statistics.

These revealed the pre-eminence, since sadly lost, of Massachusetts over other industrial states as to school laws, and labor legislation for women and children employed in factories. As early as 1876 Massachusetts had a ten-hours law for women, promptly upheld by her Supreme Court. The one permanently valuable state report was that of Carroll D. Wright, for many years chief of the Massachusetts Bureau of Labor Statistics and later

*Published in 1882 under the title, "On Some Changes in the Legal Status of the Child Since Blackstone," in the *International Review*, whose editor was Robert P. Porter, later in charge of the U.S. Census.

United States Commissioner of Labor. In it he showed incontrovertibly that in Massachusetts, after women and children were drawn into cotton textile manufacture in competition with men, the weekly earnings of father, mother and children were no more than fathers alone had previously received. Even in New York, then as now the leading industrial state, the first state factory inspector was not appointed until 1884.

The deplorable meagerness of American official information about women and children in industry led me to search the English records. The facts as they then presented themselves in the two countries afforded a firm basis for the conclusion that the future of American children depended upon the further development of steam-driven machinery and the slowly growing power of women as citizens.

This has proved true in an unforeseen and sinister sense. Little did we foresee that women in the United States would not everywhere have suffrage for nearly forty years. Still less could we anticipate that, meanwhile, the strides of industry would be so inconceivably vast that in 1920, the year of the census and of ratification of the federal suffrage amendment, more than a million children between ten and sixteen years of age would be employed. Nor could America's bitterest critic have foretold the cynical opposition which, to this day, frustrates every effort to establish for wage-earning children the equal protection of the law throughout the Republic.

In the autumn following my bachelor's degree at Cornell, I had my first experience in dealing with wage-earners. Deprived by the adverse decision of the University of Pennsylvania of the opportunity of going on with serious study while living at home, I set about starting an evening school for working girls in Philadelphia, and was given rooms for meetings by the New Century Club. This was in September, 1882. Instruction was free, chiefly bestowed by the younger members of the club. Two interesting aspects of the undertaking developed immediately. Candidates were so numerous that we overflowed before the end of the first month all available space, including stairways and halls. It soon appeared that the pupils, who were chiefly from fourteen to seventeen years old, all wished to study arithmetic and French. Most of them being department store employees, they hoped to improve their wages by learning more arithmetic, and the French language was desired as an accomplishment. Many ill-paid little growing girls went supperless twice a week, or ate two cold meals on the days when their classes met.

My share in this undertaking came to a abrupt end atThanksgiving, when my older brother was ordered to the Riviera and I was the only available person to go with him on four days notice. Fortunately, Mrs. Turner, a leading founder of the New Century Club, adopted the classes as her permanent activity, organizing them as the New Century Guild, and remained actively interested until her death, when she bequeathed it the sum of $20,000. For more than forty years it has been a useful center, combining self-government, education and recreation, having had 5,000 members since its modest beginning.

Later in the summer of Miss Anthony's London visit, Father and I journeyed by train, by carriage and on foot on the Midland countries, with a detour to Hereford. An enlightening and most agreeable episode of this journey was a visit to Albert D. Shaw,* consul at Manchester, in whose home we were entertained. From this visit I learned more than I could have gathered from dozens of volumes about protective laws then in force in England for wage-earning men, women and children. As chairman of the Committee on Ways and Means, Father was more than ever interested in what he believed to be a scientific basis for protective tariff for American industry. His formula was simplicity itself. It was the free admission of all goods that we were not prepared to produce for home consumption, and high tariff rates on all goods that we were; in order to prevent undercutting our prices through what he called "the pauper labor of Europe."

It was, therefore, for Father a startling discovery when Mr. Shaw produced evidence that hours were materially shorter for employees in English cotton-textile mills (nine hours a day and fifty-four hours a week for adults) than they were in any American state; and that the equipment of the English mills was technically so superior to that of American textile mills, even in his own Congressional district, that English employees were not materially worse off as to real wages than Father's own neighbors.

This latter statement had to be interpreted. Mr. Shaw maintained that it followed obviously from the greater purchasing power of money in England under free trade, than in America under the

*Father of Dr Henry L.K. Shaw, of Albany, former head of the American Child Hygiene Association

tariff in force in 1883. The backward state of American cotton textile industry Mr. Shaw, himself a Republican and a protectionist, attributed to the policy of excessively high rates in force in the United States.

While English textile manufacturers, subjected to the competition of France and Germany, were compelled to keep their machinery up to dateours behind their high tariff wall, could safely defer making heavy investments in improved machines. As to buildings, there was little to choose between the two countries. In both they were small and ill-lighted compared with those of today.

As a part of this pilgrimage in the Black Country, we visited the nail- and chain-makers. Their pitiful occupation was in 1910, twenty-seven years later, when minimum wage laws were first introduced in England, still one of the four most wretched employments, and was accordingly included in the new act, with box-making, the manufacture of Nottingham lace curtains, and of men's and women's ready-to-wear outer garments.

Never to be forgotten was the first of our visits in the Black Country. A poor woman working in a lean-to at the back of her two-room cottage, was hammering chains on an anvil. The raw material was brought to her by a man driving a wagon-load to be distributed throughout the neighborhood, and the chains were collected and paid for by him when finished for the owner. Her tears fell on her anvil as she told us, without pausing to look up, how she had been arrested and taken before the justice of the peace, who sent her to jail for her third failure to send her children to school under the compulsory education law which had then been in force thirteen years. Not until 1870 had England provided elementary education, and then not free.

Father asked why a justice sent a mother of three children to jail instead of the father. She replied: "But Sir, that was an act of mercy, because he earns more than I do, and the loss to the family was less when I was sent away."

Father asked why she did not send her children to school while they were too little to work and help her. She said: "I could not earn enough to pay the fees and give them porridge even without milk, and I dared not send them empty. I tried giving food and the fee to one and keeping two at home, but that broke the law too, and nothing was gained." This cruelty continued several years until the scandal became so great that fees were abolished, the justices having refused to enforce them.

There was no limit to the hours of work when the unhappy women had material and the order had to be rushed.

The owners kept wages at the lowest conceivable notch by lengthening the lists of workers and pitting them against each other. We were told by one woman after another that the uniform answer of the bringer of the raw material to complaints of the workers was, "If you don't want this work, there's plenty that does."

From 1883 until 1910 no effective step was taken in England to improve these industrial conditions, which furnished Father during the remnant of his life evidence of the evil working of free trade carried to its ultimate possible limit, with no restraint upon the "sweating" employers. He had, I learned, converted himself to protection many years before in a debate in which he had undertaken to defend free trade; and every social or industrial wrong in England directly or indirectly attributable to free trade had an abiding fascination for him.

During the campaign in England for control of sweating by a minimum-wage law, the cry of employers was that tens of thousands of working people would starve if it were passed because industry would be driven wholesale out of the country. What happened, however, was that the worst known quality of worthless hand-made chains, produced solely for export, gradually vanished from English trade and the women who had made them worked thereafter upon the next better quality of chain, and earned a minimum livelihood in contrast with the unhappy mother—a type of thousands of home-workers—whom we had seen at work upon this trash.

Here in the Black Country I first saw life under the sweating system, under free trade, under capitalism. I was to come to close quarters with it later behind our American protective tariff, under equally unrestrained capitalism. Thirteen years after our pilgrimage Victoria, Australia, made in 1896 the first successful experiment in control of the sweating system by means of minimum-wage laws which restrain the capitalist employer from operating below levels which the community sanctions. This procedure has now spread in various forms throughout all industrially developed countries, free trade and protectionist alike, except our own where it has been temporarily checked since April, 1923, by the reactionary decision of the United States Supreme Court in the District of Columbia minimum-wage case.

The old debate between English free traders and American tariff devotees in so far as it hinged on overwork and underpay of workers at the bottom levels of industry, was shown to be unreal; neither had supplied a remedy. Instead, from the youngest and farthest flung of the Anglo-Saxon commonwealths came this constructive proposal of a new type of protective legislation within the sphere of internal government.

In September 1883, following our visit to the Midlands, Mother, my brother Albert, and I journeyed to Zurich, where he attended school and I entered the university.

We had visited Oxford, but found little offered to an American woman student. Incidentally I lost, at Rugby Junction, on the Oxford trip, my trunk containing my Cornell degree. I saw it put off the train and besought the guard to put it back; but it was left there, and I never recovered it. The loss of the degree caused anxiety because it might lead to refusal to admit me as a student at Zurich, or to a delay of several months.

At the Polytechnicum, the Swiss equivalent for dean was Herr Pedell, and this functionary was as immobile as any English beadle celebrated by Dickens. Anxiously I laid before him my bereft state without my Cornell degree, and asked whether I might perhaps be present at lectures as a listener; while waiting the long time required before the issuance of a duplicate degree by Cornell. Slowly he replied:

"You may listen and you may study. When you are ready, you may present yourself for examination. An American degree has no value." I listened and studied, but never presented myself for a degree.

My absence from the United States lasted about four years. While a student I translated and, with the author's permission, later published in New York the first of that long series of studies of English industrial conditions covering more than three quarters of a century (beginning in 1844), of which the latest is a massive work entitled *Wages and the State.** Incidentally our contemporary

*Published in 1926 by P. S. King and Son, for E. M. Burns assistant in the Department of Economics of the London School of Economics.

author points out that necessary legislation, providing facilities for minimum-wage rates, has nowhere encountered such difficulties as in the United States through judicial interference.

The slender volume that I translated in 1884 in Zurich was entitled *The Condition of the Working Class in England in 1844*, by Friedrich Engels, a German whose adult life was spent in England closely identified as an eminently successful manufacturer with the textile industry and, while both lived, with Karl Marx.

When the first book appeared in 1844, in Germany in the German language, Engels was not yet twenty-four years old. Published almost half a century before Charles Booth's monumental work on *The Life and Labor of the People in London*, it is an amazing achievement, a museum specimen of painstaking, laborious, precise observation set forth in language so vivid that a Frenchman of high literary standing could hardly have excelled its clarity. It takes nothing from the value of his portrayal of facts as they then were, that a youth picturing in his first book conditions which he saw, that were incident to the Industrial Revolution in England and are now universally recognized as having been unbearable, ventured upon prophecies which have not been fulfilled in England.

Great English philanthropists, Lord Shaftesbury first of all, have one after another confirmed Engels' statements of facts. Our conservative American university libraries have slowly added to their shelves this foundation work of descriptive social and industrial history. It has been reference reading in more than one institution of the higher learning. Issued in English, in London, by Swan, Sonnenschein in 1887, it has appeared in successive editions. The author I saw but once. That was in London on our way to America.

Zurich in those days was a small and simple city, with many steep and narrow streets, some of them beautifully curved, and lined with impressive remnants of old walls. There was abundant music, and a little repertory theater subsidized by the city. The forest, owned by the canton and maintained according to the highest standards of forestry then known, extended down from the top of the Zurichberg almost to the Polytechnicum. It was an enchanting forest with broad allees cut as fire safeguards, and between the endless rows of pines, wild flowers such as I had never seen. Here we students walked by the hour arguing in English, French or German. For me, conversation in Russian was a dead loss because I have never succeeded in learning the language.

From the edge of the woods there was visible on every clear day a group of snowcaps, since, alas! concealed at that height by apartment houses, Zurich having become Switzerland's most important commercial center. Then, however, it was a joke among the polyglot students that the Russians were so busy with the future that they never knew whether the snowcaps were clear and lovely or shrouded in fog, any beauty that survived despite our modern capitalist civilization being unworthy their notice.

Like all Continental universities then and now, the Polytechnicum was without dormitories. It had no drinking and dueling clubs like the German Burschenschaften, nor fraternities or sororities. There were no boat races or other athletics, though Lake Zurich was in sight from the windows. In the vacation, some Swiss students went off with packs on their backs, tramping among their mountains or down to Italy. Barring the absence of athletics, they more than any of the others were like American students. Having no political or social grievances, and the most nearly universal educational system the world had yet seen, they shared in no political interest. They were young men gravely preparing to earn a livelihood in the professions or as technicians in business, and frankly bored by the large number of foreigners. Swiss people were the freest in the whole range of civilization. It was their proud boast that they, like England and the United States, could admit the oppressed of all the earth. How long it seems since we withdrew from that noble companionship and made the name of Ellis Island a horror!

The women students were almost all Russians, candidates for degrees in medicine and the sciences. There had been one American woman graduate in medicine, Dr. Culbertson from Boston. A Swiss, Dr. Marie Kempin, enjoyed an already growing practice in Zurich. Dr. Anita Augsburg, from Bavaria, was a candidate in the faculty of law; with a Zurich degree she became a lifelong, active suffragist in her own country. Two very beautiful and talented Russian sisters were studying, one medicine, the other chemistry, intending to come to America; a third sister was studying medicine in Berne. The only American woman student beside myself was Frances Mitchell, a Philadelphian, in the Faculty of Philosophy, who married Dr. Hans Froelicher, a fellow student, and like him was for many years on the faculty of Goucher College.

Among the Continental students I met occasionally a Viennese, a man of brilliant gifts, in the late thirties. His childhood had been one of bitter desolation. He had been boarded out by his guardian in the home of a poor shoemaker, and fed almost exclusively on potatoes and goat's milk, this meager diet registering in his slender physique and conspicuous predisposition to tuberculosis. He described plaintively his badgered existence between the Austrian police, through whom he received a pension as the illegitimate son of a noble at the Court of Franz Josef and, on the other hand, the Austrian Socialists, by writing pamphlets and editorials for whom he eked out the meager insufficiency of that loathed pension. The Socialists seemed to him so unreasonable that he withdrew more than once from their activities, only to be driven back by the chicanery of the Austrian police. Nowhere could he find rest for his soul.

There was also a Russian exile, a student of chemistry who translated Marx, put his manuscript into a small trunk and traveled as far as Freiburg on his homeward way. While he was gone to the consul to get his passport viseed, the landlord pried open the trunk and turned over to the Russian consul the manuscript intended for the underground press. The student was forthwith arrested, delivered to the Russian police and thrown into the Peter and Paul fortress, held there several years and sent to Siberia. Ultimately he escaped and crossed Bering Strait. Having acquired in prison an excellent command of English, he quickly found work as chemist in the Board of Health of a city in the Middle West where he remained for many years a much respected official. I was astonished to meet him in the course of my duties as chief state factory inspector, in Illinois in the "nineties."

Coming to Zurich, the content of my mind was tinder awaiting a match. Stowed in it were those earliest serene childhood experiences, and the tragic oppression of the recently emancipated Negroes, by disfranchisement and lynching. There were pictures of pasty-faced little working children in jail-like textile mills in Manayunk, whom I saw in the streets year after year as I drove in the phaeton between my homes in West Philadelphia and German-town. In England, only a few weeks before, there had been the pitiable toiling mothers in the chain-makers' cottages, and the diminutive men and women in the streets of the textile manufacturing cities of the Black Country. All these were baffling, human problems; and now here in Zurich among students from many lands, was the philosophy of Socialism, its assurance flooding the minds of youth and the wage-earners with hope that, within the inevitable development of modern industry, was the coming solution.

Of this I had had two stimulating foretastes before leaving America. In my sophomore year I was at home several weeks because of illness. Beside our own invalid we had with us a friend from a western city, convalescent but compelled to remain in Philadelphia for rest and observation. My duties were chiefly to play third at dummy whist, and to keep our crippled guest from going home before his cure was complete. For me Mr. Livingston was a visitor from Mars. As an importer of fine laces he was in constant contact with several foreign countries, making business journeys thither at what were then short intervals. His father had been a friend of Karl Marx and when the First International, rent by inner dissension, had had its headquarters transferred to Hoboken to save it from suppression by European governments, Mr. Livingston had taken a languid interest in it. Just before his accident he had purchased, partly as curiosities, sample pamphlets printed in English on cheap paper in bad type, and bound in flaming paper covers.

By way of inciting a discussion he urged me to read these queer looking pamphlets. They were as startling to me, a sophomore, as my discovery had been years before of the reason Grandaunt Sarah ate no sugar and always wore linen. (Sugar and cotton were products of slave labor.) Here were ideas and ideals undreamed of, and the headquarters of this world movement was as near as Hoboken!

When I went back to Cornell and the invalids resumed their normal lives, Mr. Livingston presented us gifts of lasting value in memory of that winter, mine being Vasari's *Lives of the Painters*. Keenly as I appreciated being expected to interest myself in the painters, his abiding influence on my mind was rooted in those fugitive leaflets. Intellectually that sojourn was a profitable exchange for a share, at least, of the lost Cornell work for which I was booked. This consisted of logic, economics, the history of philosophy, and the philosophy of history, the whole vast complex of learning set forth in four small square black books, especially prepared for our students by a superannuated minister who purported to elucidate all four subjects.

The other foretaste of Zurich was a lecture on Bismarck in my last term at Cornell. President White, recently returned from Berlin a devoted admirer of the creator of the German Empire, lectured to the seniors on current history in Europe. Incidentally he interpreted Socialism which the Iron Chancellor was striving to repress by methods that the German workers characterized as "sugar and the knout." The various forms of insurance against old age, sickness and industrial injuries they called "sugar" and the suppression of the Socialist press and political meetings they called the "knout." I do not know who would have been more astonished, Bismarck or Marx, at the picture of Socialism presented to our imagination! It was as follows:

"This class comes, I assume, from families whose heads are more or less responsible for carrying on the activities of the people of this state, the professions, agriculture, the industries, education, the press, transportation, and manufacture. Now if Socialism were introduced here, your fathers would be deprived of all that. It would all be handed over to the legislature at Albany." So unsophisticated were we that not one question was asked!

President White's interpretation and Mr. Livingston's pamphlets were tangents in my intellectual background on entering the Polytechnicum at Zurich to study law. The Socialist press, driven out of Germany, had headquarters in Zurich, and thither came frequently leaders of the movement who were members of the Reichstag.

An early experience was my first attendance at a Socialist meeting. It was in the old part of the city, on the second floor of a modest little eating-place, permanently so clean that one could literally have eaten off the floor. As I took my seat I was so trembling with excitement that I grasped the sides of my chair and held them firmly, for the speaker was Eduard Bernstein, then exiled editor of the organ of the German Socialist Party, several leaders of which were also present; and here was I in the World of the Future!

The subject was Bismarck's proposed high tariff for Germany. The room was filled by about twenty students from a dozen countries, and rather more skilled wage-earners, men and women in the textile and railroad industries centered in Zurich.

Before midnight every aspect of the tariff that I had ever heard or read of was presented, plus one which was utterly new to me, as a serious middle-aged Swiss railroad man argued: "There is an objection that has not been mentioned. We are internationalists; we are intimately acquainted with the textile industries; we should not fail to consider the effect on the producers of raw silk in the Orient that the tariff will involve, if prices of silk products in Germany are to be raised. The livelihood of the producers of raw silk in China and Japan will obviously have to be crowded down at least enough to meet the tariff charges in German custom houses. As internationalists, should we give our assent to this lowering of the standard of living of fellow workers on the other side of the globe?''

This might well have been a Quaker meeting. Here was the Golden Rule! Here was Grandaunt Sarah!

My eager plunge into the enthusiasm of the new movement that was beginning to kindle throughout all Europe did not blind me to certain fundamental differences. Mine was after all an American background; those youthful years of talk with Father had whetted whatever discernment Nature had given me and those differences were to determine my later thinking.

I was, however, not to turn directly from my novitiate in American and European universities to a part in the intellectual life of my generation, nor the political, nor the economic life. Instead, having married a Russian physician, I returned to America in 1886 with him and my elder son, and the ensuing five years were devoted to domestic life.

HULL-HOUSE BULLETIN

PUBLISHED AT 335 SOUTH HALSTED STREET, CHICAGO, ILL. TELEPHONE MONROE 70

| Vol. VI. | MID-WINTER, 1903-4 | No. 1 |

OBJECT OF HULL-HOUSE (as stated in its Charter): To provide a center for a higher civic and social life: to institute and maintain educational and philanthropic enterprises, and to investigate and improve the conditions in the industrial districts of Chicago.

ENTERTAINMENTS IN THE AUDITORIUM.

SUNDAY EVENING LECTURES.

Illustrated by stereopticon. 8 p. m. at the Hull-House Auditorium. Admission free.

Nov. 1—**India.** Mr. Fleming.

Nov. 8—**Italy.** Miss Hamilton.

Nov. 15—**The English Lake Country.** Miss Myra Reynolds.

Nov. 22—**American Sculpture.** Mr. Lorado Taft.

Nov. 29—**Beautiful Japan.** Dr. Toyokichi Iyenaga, University of Chicago.

Dec. 6—**The Alcestes of Euripides** (recital). Prof. R. G. Moulton, University of Chicago.

Dec. 13—**The Antigone of Sophocles** (recital). Prof. S. H. Clark, University of Chicago.

Dec. 20—**The People of the Slavic World.** Prof. E. A. Steiner, University of Chicago.

Dec. 27.—**The Messiah,** by the Evanston Choral Society.

Jan. 3—**The Holy Land.** Prof. Shailer Matthews.

The following course of six illustrated lectures on Economic Geography, by Prof. Goode, University of Chicago:

Jan. 10—**The Iron Industry.**

Jan. 17—**The Lumber Industry.**

Jan. 24—**Our Largest Cereal Crop—Corn.**

Jan. 31—**The Economic Significance of the Great Plains.**

Feb. 7—**Cotton as a Social Factor.**

Feb. 14—**The Reclamation of the Arid Lands.**

The following course of six lectures on the Capitals of Europe, by Prof. Raymond, University of Chicago:

Feb. 21—**Madrid**

Feb. 28—**Brussels.**

March 6—**Rome.**

March 13—**Copenhagen.**

March 20—**Berne.**

March 27—**Athens.**

AUDITORIUM ENTERTAINMENTS.

Oct. 14 — 8 p. m. — **Neighborhood Party,** given by Hull-House Woman's Club. Admission by invitation.

Oct. 16 — **Reception and Dance,** Men's Club Foot Ball Team.

Oct. 17 — **Reception and Dance,** Washington Irving Club.

Oct. 19 — **Reception,** given by Industrial Committee of Hull-House Woman's Club to Union Label League.

Oct. 23 — **Dancing Party,** Ida Wright Club.

Oct. 24 — **Dancing Party,** Gernon Club.

Oct. 25, 4 p. m. — **Concert.**

Oct. 30— **Dance,** Lincoln Social Club.

Oct. 31— **Dance,** Hull-House Men's Club.

Nov. 1, 4 p. m. — **Concert.**

Nov. 4 — **Reunion and Dance,** Henry Learned Club.

Nov. 6 — **Dancing Party,** Athos Club.

Nov. 13 — **Dancing Party,** Fleur de Lis Club.

Nov. 14 — **Dance,** Men's Club Foot Ball Team.

Nov. 16 — **Lecture,** by Judge Dunne, on "Municipal Ownership," under auspices of Nineteenth Ward Improvement Association.

Nov. 20 — **Neighborhood Party,** given by Hull-House Woman's Club. Admission by invitation.

Nov. 21 — **Buddhism and Buddhist Art,** Prof. Paul Caros, under the auspices of Ethical Culture Society.

Nov. 23, 8 p. m. — **Hull-House Woman's Club Harvest Home Party,** for benefit of Woman's Club Chorus. Admission, 15 cents.

Nov. 26 — **Greek Reception,** followed by stereopticon lecture on "Greece," by Miss Harriet A. Boyd.

Nov. 28 — **Afternoon,** meeting of Smith College Alumnæ.

8 p. m — **Dance,** Hull-House Men's Club.

Nov. 29, 4 p. m. — **Concert.**

Nov. 30, 8 p. m. — **Play,** "School," by Hull-House Dramatic Association. Admission, 25 cents.

PORTRAIT OF FLORENCE KELLEY AROUND 1920

I Go to Work

O n a snowy morning between Christmas 1891 and New Year's 1892, I arrived at Hull House, Chicago, a little before breakfast time, and found there Henry Standing Bear, a Kickapoo Indian, waiting for the front door to be opened. It was Miss Addams who opened it, holding on her left arm a singularly unattractive, fat, pudgy baby belonging to the cook, who was behindhand with breakfast. Miss Addams was a little hindered in her movements by a super-energetic kingergarten child, left by its mother while she went to a sweatshop for a bundle of cloaks to be finished.

We were welcomed as though we had been invited. We stayed, Henry Standing Bear as helper to the engineer several months, when he returned to his tribe; and I as a resident seven happy, active years until May 1, 1899, when I returned to New York City to enter upon the work in which I have since been engaged as secretary of the National Consumers' League.

I cannot remember ever again seeing Miss Addams hold a baby, but that first picture of her gently keeping the little Italian girl back from charging out into the snow, closing the door against the blast of wintry wind off Lake Michigan, and tranquilly welcoming these newcomers, is as clear today as it was at that moment.

Henry Standing Bear had been camping under a wooden sidewalk which surrounded a vacant lot in the nighborhood, with two or three members of his tribe. They had been precariously employed by a vendor of a hair-improver, who had now gone into bankruptcy leaving his employees a melancholy Christmas holiday. Though a graduate of a government Indian school, he had been trained to no way of earning his living and was dreadful human commentary upon Uncle Sam's treatment of his wards in the Nineties.

At breakfast on that eventful morning, there were present Ellen Gates Starr, friend of many years and fellow-founder of Hull House with Jane Addams; Jennie Dow, a delightful young volunteer kindergartner, whose good sense and joyous good humor found for her unfailing daily reward for great physical exertion. She spent vast energy visiting the homes of her Italian pupils, persuading their mothers to remove at least two or three times during the winter their layers of dresses, and give them a thorough sponge-bath in the sympathetic and reassuring presence of their kinder-gartner, Mary Keyser, who had followed Miss Addams from the family home in Cedarville and throughout the remainder of her life relieved Miss Addams of all household care. This was a full-time professional job where such unforeseen arrivals as Henry Standing Bear's and mine were daily episodes in the place which Miss Addams' steadfast will has made and kept, through war and peace, a center of hospitality for people and for ideas.

Julia Lathrop, then recently appointed county visitor for Cook County for those dependent families who received outdoor relief in money or in kind, was mentioned as away for the holidays with her family at Rockford, Illinois. Miss Lathrop, later a member of the Illinois State Board of Charities and from 1912 to 1921 through its first nine creative years, chief of the Children's Bureau at Washington, was then and is now a pillar of Hull House. Two others of the permanent group were Edward L. Burchard, for many years curator of the Field Museum; and Anna Farnsworth, an agreeable woman of leisure and means, happy to be hostess-on-call to some and all who appeared at the front door from breakfast until midnight seven days a week. That was before the squalid, recent social convention had been set up, according to which everyone, however abundant and well-assured her income, must earn her own living or be censured as a parasite. Miss Farnsworth's gracious gifts of free time and abundant good will for counseling perplexed immigrants, finding comfortable quarters for old people who could do a little work but not fend for themselves in the labor market, providing happy Saturdays in the parks for little groups of schoolchildren whose mothers worked away from home, were among the Settlement's early enrichments of the neighborhood life.

Reaching Hull House that winter day was no small undertaking. The streets between car-track and curb were piled mountain-high with coal-black frozen snow. The street-cars, drawn by horses, were frequently blocked by a fallen horse harnessed to a heavily laden wagon. Whenever that happened, the long procession of vehicles stopped short until the horse was restored to its feet or, as sometimes occurred, was shot and lifted to the top of the snow, there to remain until the next thaw facilitated its removal.

Nor were these difficulties in the way of travel minimized by free use of the telephone. In all weathers and through all depths of snow and slush and sleet, we used to navigate across Halsted Street, the thirty-miles-long thoroughfare which Hull House faced, to a drug store where we paid ten cents a call, stood throughout the process, and incidentally confided our business to the druggist and to any English-speaking neighbors who might happen in.

A superb embodiment of youth in the Mississippi Valley was Mary Kenney. Born in Keokuk, Iowa, of Irish immigrant parents, she had moved with her mother to a nearby brick tenement house, a distinguished three-story edifice in that region of drab one- and two-story frame cottages, in order to be a close neighbor to Hull House and participate in its efforts to improve industrial conditions. Her volunteer work was with self-supporting, wage-earning young women whom she hoped to form into powerful, permanent trade unions. Tall, erect, broad-shouldered, with ruddy face and shining eyes, she carried hope and confidence whithersoever she went. Her rich Irish voice and friendly smile inspired men, women and children alike to do what she wished. Her undertakings prospered and throve.

A highly skilled printer, she was employed by a company which gave preference to union employees. As a numberer she earned fourteen dollars a week, supporting herself and her lovely old mother on that wage. Hers was the initiative in making of the brick tenement a cooperative house for working girls known as the Jane Club, a large part of the success of which was for many years due to the gentle sweetness of Mrs. Kenney, who mothered the cooperators as though they had been her own.

Although this was an entirely self-governing undertaking, Miss Addams was elected year after year an honorary director, having underwritten the experiment from the beginning. Later a friend of the Settlement, as a first step towards an endowment, paid for a building planned for the convenience of the cooperators, the rent going to Hull House. This became a model for the Eleanor Clubs and countless other coooperative home clubs for self-supporting women scattered over the great city and growing with its growth during the past quarter-century.

My first activity, begun that week, was conducting for a few months a small experimental employment office for working girls and women. It was a tiny space in a corner of the building then adjoining Hull House, occupied as a morgue and undertaking establishment by an Irish-American mentioned with respect in the neighborhood because he was rumored to have various cripples and two deaths to his credit.

It soon turned out that both employers and applicants for domestic work were too few in the Hull House region to afford a basis for a self-supporting employment office. Yet finding work for people of every conceivable qualification, from high federal and state offices to rat-catching, forms a continuing chapter in the history of the House. But this has never been commercial.

In my first year at Hull House, Carroll D. Wright, U.S. Commissioner of Commerce and Labor, in charge of a federal study of the slums of great cities, entrusted me with the Chicago part of the enquiry. With a group of schedule-men under my guidance, we canvassed a square mile extending from Hull House on the west to State Street on the east, and several long blocks south. In this area we encountered people of eighteen nationalities.

Hull House was, we soon discovered, surrounded in every direction by home-work carried on under the sweating system. From the age of eighteen months few children able to sit in high-chairs at tables were safe from being required to pull basting threads. In the Hull House kindergarten children used with pleasure blunt, coarse needles for sewing bright silk into perforated outlines of horses, dogs, cats, parrots, and less known creatures on cards. They did this in the intervals between singing, modeling and playing active games. At home they used equally coarse sharp needles for sewing buttons on garments. The contrast was a hideously painful one to witness, especially when the children fell asleep at their work in their homes.

Out of this enquiry, amplified by Hull House residents and other volunteers, grew the volume published under the title *Hull House Maps and Papers*. One map showed the distribution of the polyglot peoples. Another exhibited their incomes (taken by permission from the federal schedules) indicated in colors, ranging from gold which meant twenty dollars or more total a week for a family, to black which was five dollars or less total family income. There was precious little gold and a superabundance of black on that income map!

The discoveries as to home-work under the sweating system thus recorded and charted in 1892 (that first year of my residence) led to the appointment at the opening of the legislature of 1893, of a legislative commission of inquiry into employment of women and children in manufacture, for which Mary Kenney and I volunteered as guides. Because we knew our neighborhood, we could and did show the commissioners sights that few legislators had then beheld; among them unparalleled congestion in frame cottages which looked decent enough, though drab and uninviting, under their thick coats of soft coal soot. One member of the commission would never enter any sweatshop, but stood in the street while the others went in, explaining that he had young children and feared to carry them some infection.

This commission had been intended as a sop to labor and a sinecure, a protracted junket to Chicago, for a number of rural legislators. Our overwhelming hospitality and devotion to the thoroughness and success of their investigation by personally conducted visits to sweatshops, though irksome in the extreme to the lawgivers, ended in a report so comprehensive, so readable, so surprising that they presented it with pride to the legislature. We had offered it to them under the modest title, *Memorandum for Legislative Commission of 1893*. They renamed it. The subject was a new one in Chicago. For the press the sweating system was that winter a sensation. No one was yet blase.

With backing from labor, from Hull House, from the Henry Demarest Lloyds and their numberless friends, the Commission and the report carried almost without opposition a bill applying to manufacture, and prescribing a maximum working day not to exceed eight hours for women, girls and children, together with child labor safeguards based on laws then existing in New York and Ohio, and quite advanced. There was a drastic requirement in the interest of the public health that tenement houses be searched for garments in process of manufacture, and goods found exposed in homes to contagious diseases be destroyed on the spot. Owners of goods produced under the sweating system were required to furnish to the inspectors on demand complete lists of names and addresses of both contractors and home-workers.

The bill created a state factory inspection department on which was conferred power, with regard to tenement-made goods found on infected premises, unique in this country in 1893. Illinois changed, at a single stride, from no legislation restricting working hours in manufacture for men, women or children, by day, by night, or by the week, to a maximum eight-hour day for girls and for women of all ages, in all branches of manufacture.

Hospitality akin to that of Hull House, established long before Miss Addams made her home in Chicago, was still practiced in 1892 and many years thereafter, sixteen miles out on the north shore of Lake Michigan, at Winnetka. This was in the home of Henry Demarest Lloyd and Jessie Bross Lloyd, his wife. Their house, the home life within which is an exquisite memory, stood on high ground facing eastward toward the lake, across a sloping field. The outlook was symbolic.

Thither Miss Addams convoyed me the day after my arrival at Hull-House, and there my three city-bred children and their nurse spent the rest of their first western winter, well and happy under Mrs. Lloyd's wise, unwearied kindness and exhilarated by unimagined experiences of country freedom and outdoor winter play. When spring came it was possible to install them comfortably, and well cared for, close to the little Winnetka day-school where the sons of the Lloyd family had made the change from home teaching to school. Winnetka was within easy commuting distance, and I was in constant touch with my bairns. That thrice-blest winter began for us friendships which, like those born of my Cornell experience, continue in the third generation.

Mr. Lloyd was preparing his work, published in 1894, on *Wealth Against Commonwealth*, the epoch-making beginning of the long series of enquiries into the social and industrial effects of great monopolies of our natural resources. He was already gathering material for his later volume *Newest England: Notes of a Democratic Traveler in New Zealand*, and for several others. He carried on a continuous international correspondence, with students of the incipient transition toward the present phase of the world-wide struggle for democracy in industry, for democratic control of government, for the collective spirit in human affairs.

Delicate, sensitive, reticent, a student a man of letters, Mr. Lloyd had suffered deeply during the horrors of the Haymarket trials. He saw clearly that the iniquitous precedent must distort the course of the law in Illinois for generations to come. The remnant of his life was animated by zeal to make available to the American people the experience of other nations in removing remediable evils such as, when not remedied, lead to anarchy and Communism.

Within the world-wide circle of friends and acquaintances of the Lloyd household was Governor John Peter Altgeld. When the new law took effect, and its usefulness depended upon the personnel prescribed in the text to enforce it, Governor Altgeld offered the position of chief inspector to Mr. Lloyd, who declined it and recommended me. I was accordingly made chief state inspector of factories, the first and so far as I know, the only woman to serve in that office in any state.

There had been suspiciously little opposition in the press or the legislature while our drastic bill was pending. It had passed both houses, and was signed by Governor Altgeld fairly early in the spring. Indeed the enactment of this measure, destined to be a milestone in the national history of our industry and our jurisprudence, was almost unnoticed. For this absence of timely opposition the reasons are interesting and significant.

Illinois still thought of itself as agricultural, although it ranked then as it does today, third among manufacturing states when measured by the value of its output. But neither manufacture nor the entrance therein of women and girls monopolized the imagination of Illinois in 1893. Nearly every American-born family in Chicago owned a farm in the background, in Illinois, Indiana, Iowa or Kentucky.

Illinois was, in fact, a state and Chicago was a city chiefly of men's industries, Chicago being then as now the predominant, vast, unique, inland center of freight transportation by lake and rail in this hemisphere. Illinois coal and Minnestoa iron had long since been united by great corporations to produce steel, the employees being, of course, exclusively men and boys. Rapid development of agricultural machinery (plows, reapers and threshers) was as natural as the growth of a whole city of Pullman carshops, now incorporated with Chicago, or as the stockyards.

The growing, important and permanent part played by women in Illinois industry was not widely recognized, although their role in Elgin, a city already famed for watches, was an indispensable one. Not less so was it in the vast, ever-expanding Chicago Western Electric works which rivaled the World's Fair as an attraction for foreign visitors, European and Oriental alike. The needle trades, though well started, hardly promised their present dimensions, and the typewriter was just beginning to introduce women and girls to the offices where commerce, wholesale and retail, was so soon to become preeminently the field of their activities.

The only child labor law was a city ordinance of Chicago prohibiting the employment of any child below the age of ten years at any gainful occupation, unless it had dependent upon it a decrepit adult relative. So no one had been annoyed by any law akin to ours.

Chicago, the undisputed center of finance, commerce and manufacture in the Mississippi Valley, was itself hardly aware that the problems of labor were inevitably permanent and integral in its life for generations to come.

The Haymarket riot, followed in 1887 by the hanging of the Anarchists, the Pullman strike, the great ensuing railroad strike of 1894, with the regular army patrolling the Post Office, and soldiers traveling on mail-trains, were treated as they came along, by the press, the public and the government, not as a series of vitally significant occurrences incidental to the sudden, overwhelmingly rapid development of capitalism in this vast rural area; they were treated as disagreeable episodes to be ended somehow and forgotten as quickly as possible.

As for social palliatives or preventives for injustice, hardship and labor disturbances, there were none. Workmen's compensation was not yet under discussion. It did not arrive for twenty years. The Illinois Constitution of 1872 forbade the payment of more than $5,000 for a life. It was actually cheaper to kill a worker than to injure one, because the jury might vote punitive damages to the injured person.

The final decisive reason for the bewildering absence of contemporary hostility to the enactment of the Illinois factory law of 1893 was probably the universal indifference to enforcement of laws of any kind. A statute was put on the books and nothing happened. Or if an attempt at enforcement was made, the State Supreme Court was relied upon to annul the law. Or the ensuing legislature repealed it.

This latter fate had befallen a compulsory education law enacted by the legislature of 1891, requiring instruction in English in all schools throughout the state. After a virulent political campaign this measure was wiped out by the legislature of 1893. The feeling was, however, very strong that something must be done for the children. Our provision that they could not be employed for wages in manufacture before the fourteenth birthday or longer than eight hours, or at night, or without a certificate, was for this reason not wholly unwelcome.

My appointment dated from July 12, 1893. The appropriation for a staff of twelve persons was $12,000 a year, to cover salaries, traveling expenses, printing, court costs, and rent of an office in Chicago. The salary scale was, for the Chief $1500 a year; for the first assistant, also a woman, Alzina P. Stevens $1000; and for each of the ten deputies of whom six were men $720. Needless to say this had been voted by a legislature predominantly rural.

It was Governor Altgeld's definite intent to enforce to the uttermost limit this initial labor law throughout his term of office. He was a sombre figure; the relentless hardship of his experience as a boy and youth had left him embittered against Fate, and against certain personal enemies, but infinitely tender towards the sufferings of childhood, old age and poverty. He was an able, experienced lawyer, and his sense of justice had been outraged by the conduct of the trial of the Anarchists. Indeed, no one yet knows who threw the fatal bomb in the Haymarket riots. The men who were hanged were charged with conspiracy to do a deed of which no one has ever known the actual doer. All the evidence against them was circumstantial, and in this respect the trial is, so far as I know, still unique in the history of American jurisprudence, the only trial closely resembling it in any considerable degree being that of the Molly Maguires in the mining regions of Pennsylvania in the early seventies of the nineteenth century. To Governor Altgeld's mind the whole Illinois retributive procedure presented itself as terrorism.

To the personnel of the newly created department for safe-guarding women and children who must earn their living in manufacture, Governor Altgeld showed convincingly a passionate desire to use every power conferred for the benefit of the most inexperienced and defenseless elements in industry in Illinois.

My first effort to apply the penalty for employing children below the age of sixteen years without the prescribed working paper, led me to the office of the district attorney for Cook County. This was a brisk young politician with no interest whatever in the new law and less in the fate of the persons for whose benefit it existed. The evidence in the case I laid before him was complete. An eleven-years-old boy, illegally engaged to gild cheap picture frames by means of a poisonous fluid, had lost the use of his right arm, which was paralyzed. There was no compensation law and no prohibition of work in harzardous occupations. There was only a penalty of twenty dollars for employing a child without the required certificate. The young official looked at me with impudent surprise and said in a tone of astonishment:

"Are you calculating on *my* taking this case?"

I said: "I thought you were the district attorney."

"Well," he said, "suppose I am. You bring me this evidence this week against some little two-by-six cheap picture-frame maker, and how do I know you won't bring me a suit against Marshall Field next week? Don't count on me. I'm overloaded. I wouldn't reach this case inside of two years, taking it in its order."

That day I registered as a student in the Law School of Northwestern University for the approaching fall term, and received in June 1894, a degree from that University whose graduates were automatically empowered to practice before the Supreme Court of Illinois. Credit was given for my reading law with Father in Washington in 1882, my study in Zurich, and one year in the senior class in Chicago. The lectures were given in the evening and did not interfere with my administrative work.

In Chicago, in the winter and spring and summer of 1893, all available public spirit and creative energy were centered upon the World's Fair. The name was not an exaggeration. World-wide publicity had brought together works of all the arts in such profusion, and of such superior quality as have never since been assembled on this continent. Like its Philadelphia predecessor, the Exposition was opened on July 4. Here was gloriously celebrated, as has been said before, the coming of age of American industry. Certainly no one who saw that marvelous achievement of art, architecture and enterprise unified for a common, noble purpose, can ever forget it.

Alas for its ephemeral effect upon the community which produced it! When it vanished, Chicago was outwardly as though the Fair had never been. A lovely vision, an entrancing mirage had come and gone. Smoke, soot, crude, uncoordinated building of clumsy structures without common plan or civic forethought, remained and long continued as they had been before the Fair. The Field Museum and the broad avenue named the Midway were exceptions that provided this rule.

Two less famous occurrences of 1893 in Chicago were the financial and industrial panic with protracted unemployment and wretched suffering, and the epidemic of smallpox which followed a neglected case on the Midway of the Exposition. These horrors carried over throughout the year 1894, and with the latter I was excitingly identified.

At the close of the Fair, the hideous fact could no longer be concealed that smallpox had been gradually spreading from the Midway to the homes of some garment workers on the West Side. It was mandatory upon us to seek, as soon as we learned this, all clothing in process of manufacture in such places and, if exposure to the presence of the infection was clearly provable, to destroy the goods on the premises. We could never learn with any approach to accuracy how nearly all of the exposed goods we ultimately found.

Daily reports to the Board of Health with requests for immediate vaccination of the exposed dwellers in tenements placarded with the yellow smallpox card, produced no results. Milkmen came and went as usual. The families of patients, vaccinated and unvaccinated alike, visited the corner grocery and went their way to the factories. Among the immigrants who were the bulk of the garment-making home-workers, the only really safe ones were those who had had smallpox in the old country, or who had been vaccinated at Ellis Island as a preliminary to admission to this country. Babies born after landing had little chance of surviving, for the vaccination ordinance was as little enforced as any other law. Many infants and little children we found concealed on closet shelves, wrapped in bundles, sometimes to keep them from being vaccinated, sometimes to keep them—with the disease so fully developed that concealment was unthinkable—from being sent to the sorely dreaded hospital. Not until Gov. Altgeld announced he was about to call a conference of the governors of Indiana, Wisconsin, Iowa, Missouri and Kentucky, with a view to instituting an embargo upon all shipments of products of the needle trades from Chicago did the owners of the goods believe that the new law must be obeyed. They then instituted in good earnest a campaign of vaccination in their factories, their contract shops, and the tenements to which these latter sent out goods. So strong was the feeling against vaccination in the tenements that one promising young surgeon working with the vaccination squad was disabled for life for his profession, his elbow being shattered by a shot from an excited tailor.

The non-transmissibility of smallpox germs in woolen fabrics seems never to have been definitely proved. Without reference to the epidemic the occasional appearance of isolated cases on lonely farms in the Northwest, throughout 1924, could not be explained, especially when it coincided, as it frequently did, with the previous receipt of woolen garments from the Chicago mail-order houses.

The Illinois Association of Manufacturers, established in 1893, seems not to have been in working order until after the new law took effect in July, or to have been too feeble to make any timely opposition. No sooner, however, had we begun to enforce the statute against violators in the tenement houses, by urging their employers to cut off supplies of work during the period of the epidemic, warning them that goods found in the presence of infection would be summarily destroyed, than many workers showed us letters from the Manufacturers' Association promising protection if they were molested by inspectors who were, the letters said, operating under a new law clearly unconstitutional.

From that day the Illinois labor law has never been without strenuous opposition, sometimes open, sometimes concealed, from that active body. When a labor measure for women or minors has been strengthened on paper, or a valuable new one enacted, the quality of the administering officials has been reduced, if this could be achieved.

This reactionary but undeniably permanent power of the Illinois Manufacturers' Association was formerly chargeable to a grievous error of the exceedingly powerful trade unions, viz: their neglect of, and contempt for, statutory safeguards compared with negotiations of the organized workers through their unions. Since 1920, however, this responsibility is shared by the rank and file of women voters who fail to line up effectively behind the most important labor measures. Together, voting women and organized voting labor could always win.

PHOTOGRAPH OF FLORENCE KELLEY, 1915
WHEN THE UNITED STATES GOVERNMENT
REFUSED HER A PASSPORT

𝒜ppendix:

The Need of Theoretical Preparation
for Philanthropic Work

Etymologically philanthropy is, of course, the love of mankind, and, at first sight, it seems superfluous to undergo theoretical preparation for expressing one's love of mankind. That seems to be wholly a matter of the heart, the sympathies, the sense of right. But experience has long shown that these qualities alone do not suffice. For man lives in society, and society has its own laws of development, an understanding of which is absolutely necessary if our philanthropic effort is not to be wasted or worse.

If, for instance, in our goodness of heart and our ignorance of the laws of development of the society in which we live, we should assume that all men are brothers, it would be only to make the painful discovery that these "brothers" are today divided into two classes engaged in a life-and-death struggle: the smaller class owning all the necessaries of life, all the means of production—houses, lands, mills, forges, furnaces, the harvests, and the ships and trains in which they are transported—in short, everything with which work can be carried on; and the larger class, the vast majority of

"The Need of Theoretical Preparation for Philanthropic Work " originally appeared in Helen Hiscock Backus, *The Need and Opportunity for College Trained Women in Philanthropic Work* (N.Y.: New York Association of Collegiate Alumnae, 1887), pp. 15-26.

these "brothers," owning nothing but their labor power, and forced to sell that piece by piece and day by day for what it will bring in the labor market. In practice, every interest of these "brothers" is and must be diametrically opposed. And if, in our want of theoretical preparation, we prefer to behave differently, a thousand proofs meet us day by day. Every strike or lockout is at bottom a class struggle. The workers will work less and have more, and the employers will pay less and have more, and each side *must*, in the struggle for self-preservation, assume the attitude it does assume. But not in the labor market only is the class struggle forced upon our attention. In the church, the priest who speaks his honest conviction in the interests of the workers is "isolated" by the hierarchy; in politics, the man who stands forth as their standard-bearer is covered with ridicule, branded the enemy of order and civilization, a crank, and whatever epithet seems most opprobrious; while, before the law, a striker—the worker—is liable to imprisonment for conspiracy; the employer—the capitalist who locks out his men has yet to be molested in this State.

One consequence of the division of society into two warring classes is this: that there are two sorts of philanthropy. There is our bourgeois philanthropy, to which we college graduates are born and bred; and there is the philanthropy of the working class, which differs radically from our own.

I shall try, first, to make clear the nature and limitations of our bourgeois philanthropy; and then I shall try to make clear the nature of the philanthropy of the workers. And if I succeed in doing this, the need of theoretical preparation for philanthropic work will demonstrate itself in the process.

Our bourgeois philanthropy, whatever form it may take, is really only the effort to give back to the workers a little bit of that which our whole social system, systematically, robs them of, and so to prop up that system yet a little longer.

It is the workers who produce all values; but the lion's share of what they produce falls to the lion—the capitalist class—and enables the capitalist arbitrarily to decide what he will do with it and whether or not he will use part of the spoils for the good of the despoiled, a part of the plunder for the good of the plundered; and, however disinterestedly individual men and women may devote themselves to this task of restitution, the fact remains that, for the capitalist class as a whole, all philanthropic effort is a work of resititution for self-preservation.

This is outspoken for the class, as a class, when our social science congresses and associated charities meetings occupy their sessions with questions of the treatment of the dependent and defective classes, with plans to minimize the danger with which these elements threaten society, by palliating such of the evils consequent upon our present system of production and distribution as philanthropy can cope with.

The dangerous classes, thieves, murderers, paupers, all of whom are as much an integral part of our social system as we college-bred women, must be restrained; epidemic disease, as murderous to the ruling class as to the workers, must be prevented in self-defense; pauperism, inevitable consequence of free competition and man-superseding machinery, must be met by industrial training, the abolition of outdoor relief, the organization of charities, all in order that the system of production and distribution which engenders all these evils may endure a little longer; and the same unconscious, unformulated self-interest finds, perhaps, the most adroit expression in the arrangement known as profit-sharing. This institution embodies bourgeois philanthropy pure and simple. According to the accepted usage of the business world, he only may share the profits of good years who can bear his share of the losses of bad ones. But the workingman, having nothing, cannot bear any losses whatsoever. So the share kindly given back to the workers out of the profits the whole of which they created, is arbitrarily determined by the employer, who thereby kills divers birds with one stone: he eases his conscience by making some slight restitution; he binds the hands to the concern by means of the trifling increase in their wages, so that they watch one another to prevent wasteful work from diminishing the share, and they are loath to strike or in any way injure the profits of which they gratefully accept the share allotted to them.

In the struggle for existence, with the labor organizations on the one hand, and powerful competitors on the other, such advantages in the alliegance of the firm's own hands are cheaply bought with the restitution of a share of the profits. And this one form of individual philanthropy I find typical of the whole. We give back a percentage and had our account in prolonging the system that gives us all the rest.

I do not for a moment lose sight of the noble self-sacrifice of men and women who, in all disinterestedness, give years of their life to philanthropic effort. Nor do I believe that all or most of such work is done with the conscious intention of propping up a system of society which is based upon the exploitation of the working class. On the contrary, it is because I am convinced of the honorable and noble intention which animates a vast part of such work, that it seems to me necessary for every thinking woman to pause before entering upon it and ask herself the question: what is the real nature of philanthropic work, and is the kind usually entered upon by the men and women of my class such as will satisfy my longing to be of use to my fellow men and women?

For our grandmothers at our age, before our present system of production had developed to its present stage, when the contrasts of class were less sharply defined, philanthropic work was simple enough: neighborly help of those less comfortably placed, or, possibly, contribution to the maintenance of some one of a few charitable institutions. For our mothers, and those of us who virtually belong to their generation, having lost step with the rapid march of industrial and social development that marks the last few years, the philanthropic problem, though complicated enough, is by no means a vital one. There is simply the choice among the thousand and one forms of philanthropic activity all more or less approved by the class to which we belong.

Accepting the social system of today as eternal, final, and the poor always with us as being incident to it, the only problem would be to minimize their number and alleviate their sufferings as far as may be. Then the only theoretical preparation possible would be a study of methods. But for the thinking women of our generation the vital question is no longer between giving doles to street beggars on the one hand, or supporting the associated charities on the other; or between the temperance, the white cross, and the suffrage movement, as to many persons it still seems to be. The question that forces itself upon us, and imperatively demands an immediate answer, is this: in the great strife of classes, in the life-and-death struggle that is rending society to its very foundations, where do I belong? Shall I cast my lot with the oppressors, content to patch and darn, to piece and cobble at the worn and rotten fabric of a perishing society? Shall I spend my life in applying palliatives, in trying to make the intolerable endurable yet a little longer? Shall I spend my youth upon a children's hospital, when the dispensary rolls of the city show that the deterioration of the child-physique in the working class is out of proportion to all that palliatives can do to check it. That increasing poverty brings increasing rachitic disease out of all proportion to the growth of population, so that hospital work is a Sisyphus task? Shall I send a score or a hundred children for recreation to the country, while year by year our factories and tenement-house workrooms demand fresh thousands of children to toil within their noisome prison walls? Shall I preach temperance to men whose homes are vile tenements, whose wives toil side by side with them because the father's wages no longer suffice to maintain the family? Men whose exhausted, ill-nourished frames demand stimulants because the wife has no time, strength, money with which to procure and prepare good and sufficient food? Shall I preach chastity to homeless men, the hopeless discomfort of whose surroundings must concentrate their whole desire upon the gratification of animal passion, while want forces scores of thousands of women to sell themselves to the first-comer? Shall I fritter away the days of my youth investigating the deservingness of this or that applicant for relief when the steady march of industrial development throws a million able-bodied workers out of employment, to tramp the country, seeking in vain a chance to earn their bread, until hundreds, aye, thousands of them, broken, discouraged, demoralized, settle down into the life of the chronic pauper?

Shall I not rather make common cause with these my brothers and my sisters to make an end of such a system?

Here lies the choice. If we stand by the class to which by education we belong, our philanthropic work, whether we will or no, must bear its stamp, being merely palliative, helping one child while the system sacrifices tens of thousands, saving one girl while thousands fall, building one hospital while every condition of our social life grows more brutally destructive of human life and health.

As loyal members of the ruling class our work must, I repeat, be merely pallative. For a radical cure of the social disease means the end of the system of exploiting the workers. But to stop exploiting would be suicide for the class that we are born and educated into, and of which we college-bred women form an integral part. Lest this should sound like mere abuse, we have but to recall to mind the origin of poverty in our society.

I need not waste words in pointing out to you that the recipients of philanthropic benefits spring from the working class, whether they are babies, who need creches because their mothers are forced to go to the factory; or free kindergartens, because the workman

has no money for school bills; or hospitals, because home nursing
is out of the question; or free transportation to the West, because
home life has been crushed out in the struggle for life itself, and the
Children's Aid Society must find a substitute for the real article; or
whether the recipient is a candidate for some home for the aged,
because wages can be earned only through the prime of life;
whatever the special case, the mass of cases come from the workers.

Women to be rescued, men to be reformed, whatever the form
of the social wreckage, it all comes from the class of the plundered.
Of course there are exceptions, as when boodle aldermen in jail are
given flowers by well-meaning women. But the exceptions do but
prove the rule that the recipients spring from the working class.
Nor is the reason far to seek, for it is a law of political economy
that the working class receives only enough of the fruits of its labor
to maintain itself and bring up the rising generation according to
the prevailing declining standard of life of the working class in the
given country at the given time, the remainder of the fruits of
labor falling to the capitalist class, by virtue of the monopoly of the
means of production held by that class. This remainder which falls
to the capitalist class is surplus value, and I must ask you to have
patience a moment while I try to explain what that is.

Under our industrial system the means of production are a
monopoly of an irresponsible class, and the workers are forced to
compete with one another for the privilege of employment in using
them. In the struggle for existence that arises out of this competition the weak go to the wall, become the wreckage that philanthrophy undertakes to deal with.

Under this competion of the workers among themselves, the
labor power of each is a commodity which he or she must sell in the
labor market for whatever price it will bring; and, like all com-
modities, this labor power has twofold value—exchange-value or
market-value and use-value. In the case of a shirtmaker, for instance, the market-value of a day's labor power may be represented
by eighty cents or whatever it will bring, whatever the manufacturer
can engage her for. But the commodity, labor power, has a unique
quality. It creates other values. So when the shirt manufacturer
buys of the shirtmaker her labor power for a day, it is in order to
set it to work producing new values. But he is very careful to see
that it produces new values beyond the eighty cents he pays for it.
Suppose he gives the shirtmaker shirting worth a dollar and in six
hours she has made shirts worth a $1.80: he has his money back (in

value, at least) that he pays her for the whole day. But he has bought her labor power for the whole day, and she must toil on; and the product of the remaining hours embodies surplus-value, value beyond the wages that represent the market-value of her day's labor. It is out of this difference between the market-value paid the shirtmaker for her day's labor power, and the value created by her in the day's work, that the manufacturer's profit comes. And if we take the whole class of workers, we must admit that this appropriation of surplus-value, this exploitation of the workers, is the source of the poverty of the working class, of its supplying wreckage to need philanthropic attention.

But any radical methods directed against this exploitation, this profit-plunder, are measures directly against the class that lives by it and to that class we belong by birth and especially by education, and this fact it is which makes us especially need theoretical preparation for philanthropic work, if that work is to be abreast of the life of our time and not run in old ruts.

For the first thing necessary is to get rid of the predjudices in which we have grown up, to see our philanthrophy as it really is, and this is especially necessary for us college bred women, because our colleges are so emphatically class institutions; the students are children of the ruling class, except in a small number of cases where scholarships help those rare exceptions among the workers' children who suceed in escaping daily drudgery for their daily bread, and by dint of all privation work their way to and through college; such scholarships are too few and too meager to make the workers' children who obtain them other than rare exceptions among their more prosperous fellow students. Moreover, the scholarships are usually mere tuition. In any case, the scholarship is the exception and the pay-student the rule—a fact which stamps the college as a class institution. But if, with one wave of change throughout the length and breath of the land, every college were thrown open wide by free tuition and every student presenting himself or herself for successful examination were admitted and supported throughout the college course, this would still change nothing of the character of the college as a class institution, for the innate majority of American youth must earn their daily bread during those years of older childhood and early youth, which the children of the ruling minority spend in preparing for college. If our colleges were thrown open tomorrow, our telegraph and messenger-boys errand-boys, door-openers, cash-girls, and the scores of thousands of mill children would never enter college. Our system of production and distribution demands their labor in increasing measure every year, and the increasing poverty of the workers makes the wages of children more essential for the maintenance of the family. The grade of society from which children may be expected to enter college becomes, therefore, more and more sharply defined.

The class character of college life may be seen, too, in the political attitude of the students. In 1848 the students stood shoulder to shoulder with the workmen on the barricades of the European cities fighting to bring the middle class to the helm against the aristocracy and despotic monarchy. And in our own country, a quarter of a century ago, the Harvard regiment marched to meet its fate in the work of freeing the slaves, so doing what students could to bring the present perfection of capitalism and class rule, since capitalism presupposes the juridical freedom of the worker, and Negro slavery hemmed its progress in America as monarchical and aristocratic reaction had hemmed it in Europe. But today, that struggle is over, the middle class rules in both hemispheres, and the whole character of its struggle has changed, becoming one long endeavor to maintain ascendancy against the oncoming forces of the workers now claiming their turn as the middle class was still claiming its own at the time of our Rebellion. The class to which we students belong has survived its honorable role as champion of freedom against oppression, and has become the defender of the day that now is, living by oppression and plunder as cynically as ever did the feudal aristocracy. And the students embody the sentiment of the class as they have always done, and placed themselves upon the side of the old parties against the rising party of labor.

Our colleges being institutions owned by the ruling class (even when founded with public money) for the training of the rising generation thereof, and manned by its carefully selected employees, the economic and sociological teaching done in them is such as the employers require, of which samples may be found in the publications of Professors Sumner, Perry, Atkinson, Thompson and others. Lest this seem too sweeping, I ask: "Where are the teachers, men or women, who have placed themselves outspokenly on the side of the oppressed class?" In medicine, in the natural sciences, the word of the day is, "Investigation regardless of consequences; the truth at all costs!" But in social science there seems always in some insidious form the misleading influence of personal or class interest. When a Dubois Reymond forgets himself so far as to declare the German universities training schools for the intellectual bodyguard of the Hohenzollerns; when Virchow raises his voice in warning against Haeckel's plan for introducing the history of evolution into the public schools, because "the Darwinian theory leads to socialism" (as though the trend of social development could be helped or hindered by teaching or not teaching a certain department of natural science in the public schools!), surely it is much to demand of the rank and file of American professors that they rise superior to tradition and all considerations of personal advantage and espouse the cause of the class that does not employ them in direct antagonism to the class that does. Nor do I accuse the rank and file of America's professors of dishonorable action. That which is unpardonable in a Virchow and a Dubois Reymond, who know whereof they speak, may be honest ignorance in the rank and file, the more so as the fundamental works of modern scientific political economy have been shut up in a foreign tongue, and are only now accessible to English readers. Fortunately the time is rapidly passing away when that excuse can be made, for the modern literature of economics is now, for the most part, translated into English, and ignorance of it will henceforth be unpardonable for the teacher. But honorably or dishonorably, ignorantly or wilfully, certain it is that we have, as a rule, been taught in our colleges to accept our present social system with the method of production that underlies it, not as a phase of development leading to a higher order, just as antique slavery gave place to serfdom of the Middle Ages, and feudalism to our capitalistic system, but as final, permanent, perhaps God-given.

The foundation of our social order being accepted, there remained for the teachers much field for critical research, and collegiate activity in the domain of economics and sociology might busy itself with subordinate questions of practical politics such as the relative merits of free trade and protection as well as with anything else. For such teaching as the prevailing textbooks present, the time allotted in the ordinary curriculum is ample: since our professors of political economy do, as a rule, but present the now threadbare propositions of the few original minds who did work of their own in the last century and earlier decades of the present one; or serve as mere apologists for the social system, the laws of whose development few of them attempt to investigate.

and the class relation vitiates the intercourse, whether we are conscious of it or not. But when we go to the meetings of the workers or join their organizations, both these vitiating influences cease to operate, and we meet them simply as students honestly seeking enlightenment.

To the end of maintaining and strengthening their own class in its struggle for the ascendancy, the workers have their own institutions for preventing workers from becoming social wreckage; their sick benefit societies, reciprocal help in times of strike and lockout, and most of all, the trades organizations. There is no element of restitution in this, their philanthropic work, in their sharing their poverty and savings. In all their reciprocal contributions and mutual benefits the emphasis belongs to the words *reciprocal* and *mutual*, the truly social idea, "each for all and all for each," the principal of active brotherhood underlying them all. Nor is their effort palliative in the sense of being calculated to prop up the system of capitalistic exploitation. On the contrary, the palliatives for which they strive, such as the shortening of the working day or the limitation of the working of children, aim heavy blows at the production of surplus-value, and would vastly conserve the strength of the workers for their struggle for the overthrow of capitalism. Nor do the workers reject any such philanthropic effort, from whatever quarter, as may contribute to maintain and strengthen their class. They accept it, the more enlightened recognizing the element of restitution, the less enlightened feeling instinctively that the workers, the creators of all values, are entitled to all and more than all the good that under our present social system falls to their lot. I shall have made clear our need of theoretical preparation for philanthropic work if I have clearly indicated the general difference between the restitution for self-preservation practiced half- unconsciously by our own class, and the reciprocal help of the workers among themselves pending their struggle for the abolition of the system under which they, and with them the whole of society, suffer.

As to the book-work to be done by way of theoretical preparation for efficient work for the elevation of the race, we Americans have had slender opportunity of becoming acquainted with the literature of modern scientific political economy, because its fundamental works have hitherto been locked up in a foreign language. We have, indeed, been at a double disadvantage in this respect, for not only were the works themselves not accessible but

I have dwelt thus at length upon the nature of our collegiate institutions and of the instruction in economics given in them,
because I wish to make clear the especial need which we college-
bred women have of theoretical preparation before we can clearly
appreciate the true nature of that bourgeois philanthropy which is
an essential evil of our society. Born and bred among class
prejudices and traditions, our college course of economic study
usually affords us either no light on the subject or actual darkness,
the teaching that should be in the direction of unprejudiced investigation being only too frequently dogmatic apology for the
social system as it is today.

Within a very short time there has, it is true, been some progress
made in the direction of critical investigation, and the appearance
of the journals founded by Harvard and Columbia for this purpose
is a symptom to be greeted with warm welcome.

For every graduate, however, who conceives philanthropic work
to mean conscientious endeavor for the real elevation of the race,
and not a mere gratification of her own goodness of heart, the need
of theoretical preparation is most urgent at the moment of leaving
college. For, her mind filled with dogmatic apology for society as it
is, the task of hearing the other side lies before her, and it is no trifling task.

This other side is the theory of the development of society, the
theory which is to political economy what the Darwinian theory is
to the natural sciences. It is the working class which naturally
espouses the theory of the development of society, and looks to the
future for improvement just as the class now in possession of all
that makes life pleasant naturally accepts the apology for society as
it is, and reveres our threadbare orthodox political economy for its
services in that direction. And this attitude of the working class,
even when it is only instinctive, makes contact with it indispensable
for the honest student of economics or of the real elevation of the
race. I do not mean by this, contact with the wreckage of the working class by means of participation in some of our thousand and
one charitable institutions or associations; still less do I mean individual almsgiving. For any contact worth having with the
workers the honest student must go to the embodiment of their
healthiest, strongest life—their labor organizations. Here only is
contact upon the basis of our common humanity possible, for we
are as a rule condemned, as members of the ruling class, to meet
our working brothers and sisters either as employers or alms-givers,

the reports upon their contents were, in too many cases, made either by men who had a direct interest in misrepresenting them, or by persons insufficiently qualified for the task, whose resumes and popularizations, though, doubtless, honorably meant, have nevertheless been misleading. Now, however, the works themselves are accessible to all who are willing to do the preliminary elementary reading requisite for understanding them.

One excellent little preliminary work is an American volume, entitled *The Cooperative Commonwealth.*[1] Though by no means a strictly scientific work, this popular essay serves as a capital introduction to the theory of social development.

Another useful preliminary work is August Bebel's *Woman in the Past, Present and Future,*[2] which is most suggestive and well worth reading, even by persons who do not propose to make any systematic study of social questions.

Having gone through these slender preliminaries, there remain the fundamental works, most of which have only now been made accessible in English—most, but not all of them, for one of the most valuable works of this literature is the creation of our fellow countryman, Lewis Morgan, the result of his forty years of research into the development of society through the stages of slavery and barbarism to civilization. *Ancient Society,*[3] the most important of his works, shows that he reached by this wholly different route the same conclusions reached by the great founder of modern scientific political economy, Karl Marx. Marx and his friend Engels have made a most brilliant popularization, elaboration and condensation of this work, under the title *Der Ursprung der Familie, des Privateirgenthums und des Staates,*[4] which is warmly to be recommended to those who read German. It will also be translated into English in the near future.

Another of the indispensable books is *The Condition of the Working Class in England*[5] by Friedrick Engels, which is especially valuable for American readers because the conditions described in it as prevailing in England at the time of its appearance in German are reproduced upon a larger scale in America now at the moment of its publication in an English translation. It is the best introduction to the study of modern scientific political economy and the fundamental work *par excellence* thereof, *Capital,*[6] by Karl Marx.

The last-named classical work has, within the past half year, been made accessible to English readers. Published in 1867 in German, it was at once translated into Russian, and, after the lapse of several years, into French; but only now, after twenty years, has it come into possession of the English-speaking peoples. It is to political economy what the works of Darwin are to the natural sciences, a theory of development and a critical investigation thereof. So great is the importance of this work, that despite the prohibition of the German Imperial Government and the enmity of professional opponents of its teachings, there is not a chair of economy in any German university whose occupant is not forced sooner or later to deal with it, while candidates for promotion in the field of economics find it their most fruitful field for critical investigation. She who has mastered this work thoroughly finds a wholly new standpoint from which to judge the society of today, with its good and its evils.

The war of the classes is seen in a new light as the struggle which can and must end only in a higher organization of society; the ever-intensifying concentration of the means of production in the hands of the few, however frightful the suffering it involves to the many, apears as the necessary transition from the haphazard production of today to the orderly work of the future. The organization of labor—that bugbear of the timid and the ignorant—is seen to be the one great hope of a peaceful transition from the wage -slavery and class-rule of today to that true democracy of the future when all shall be free, not in name only but in deed and in truth. The evils of oppression, exploitation and greed of gain on the one hand and of overwork, pauperism, disease, intemperance and the thousand and one subordinate ills our philanthropy deals with on the other, assume their true relations and proportions as integral parts, inherent qualities in a changing social system. And the real philanthropic work, the real work for the elevation of the race, the truest, highest expression of our love of mankind proves to be the task of making clear to the workers the cause of the evils under which they and, with them, the whole of society suffer, showing them where lies their strength and where their weakness, where they can work in harmony with the process of social development and where to find the point of least resistance.

For the future rests with the working class. As the civil elements of society once slowly grew to power, struggling long in vain against monarchy and aristocracy until with one mighty upheaval they threw off, in the French Revolution, the yoke of feudalism, so now the working class, slowly growing in union and power, in enlightenment and conscious will, is gathering its forces to assume the helm. However much the wreckage that our system engenders within its ranks, however great the privation, the suffering inflicted by our class-rule, the wreckage after all is only a small part of the whole vast class, while the enlightened portion of it increases with every passing day. To cast our lot with the workers, to seek to understand the laws of social and industrial development, in the midst of which we live, to spread this enlightenment among the men and women destined to contribute to the change to a higher social order, to hasten the day when all the good things of society shall be the goods of all the children of men, and our petty philanthropy of today superfluous—this is the true work for the elevation of the race, the true philanthropy. And I think that you will agree with me that before we are ready to enter upon it we have some need of theoretical preparation.

[1]*Cooperative Commonwealth*, by Laurence Gronlund. Boston, Lee & Shepard.

[2]*Woman in the Past, Present and Future*, by August Bebel. Cheap editions of both published by the John W. Lovell Publishing Co., N. Y.

[3]*Ancient Society*, by Lewis Morgan. Published by Henry Holt & Co., N. Y.

[4]*Der Ursprung der Familie, des Privateiegenthums und des Staates [Origin of the Family, Private Property and the State]*, von Friedrich Engels. Verlag der Volksbuchhhandlung, Zurich, Schweiz. May be had at 172 First Ave., N. Y.

[5]*The Condition of the Working Class in England*, by Frederick Engels. Published by the J. W. Lovell Co., New York, 1887.

[6]*Capital: A Critical Analysis of Capitalist Production*, by Karl Marx. Translated from the German by Samuel Moore and Edward Aveling. Edited by Frederick Engels. Published 1887, by Swan, Sonnenschein & Co., London.

Glossary

Addams, Jane (1860-1935). Social settlement leader, social reformer and peace activist, Jane Addams was raised in a prosperous Illinois family. Her father served eight terms as state senator, and helped Abraham Lincoln create the Republican Party in Illinois. Inspired by her father's highminded idealism and by Lincoln's legacy of social reform, Addams attended Rockford Female Seminary, graduating in 1881, the year of her father's death. For almost a decade she sought work commensurate with her ideals and her social background; after a visit to Toynbee Hall, a university settlement in London's East End, she and her friend Ellen Gates Starr decided to establish a similar settlement in Chicago. Hull House opened in 1889; Addams and Starr made it one of the most influential centers of social reform in the Western world. Many other talented women, such as Julia Lathrop and Florence Kelley, became lifelong associates of Hull House.

Devoted not to philanthropy or charitable work, but to political and social reforms to promote good citizenship and social welfare among the urban poor, Jane Addams exerted a pervasive influence within American democracy during the critical years of transformation between 1890 and 1915. Thereafter she directed her energies primarily to the cause of international peace; in 1919 she was elected the first president of the Women's International League for Peace and Freedom. In the 1920s she was denounced by the Daughters of the American Revolution, the American Legion and other conservative groups, but the esteem in which she was held by her contemporaries was symbolized in 1931 when she was awarded the Nobel Peace Prize.

Altgeld, John Peter (1847-1902). Son of a German immigrant, Altgeld was the first Democratic governor of Illinois after the Civil War. In 1886 he was elected to the superior court of Cook County (Chicago), and was chief justice in 1891 when he resigned to run for governor. His election was part of a larger pattern of Democratic victories that reelected Grover Cleveland. A few months after his inauguration Altgeld ruined his political future by pardoning three anarchist prisoners convicted of murdering policemen during the Haymarket affair of 1886. (Four others had already been hanged and another had committed suicide in his cell.) Altgeld was convinced that the men had not received a fair trial and were almost certainly innocent; historians have tended to support his conclusion, but the influential media of his own time branded him a revolutionary and even an anarchist. In 1894 Altgeld opposed President Cleveland's action in sending U.S. army troops to maintain "order" during the Pullman strike.

Ames, Charles Gordon (1828-1912). A Baptist and later a Unitarian clergyman, Ames became pastor of the Unitarian Church in Germantown, Pennsylvania in 1872. In response to the hardships among the poor during the depression winter of 1873, he helped form one of the first organized charitable societies in the U.S.

Anthony, Susan Brownell (1820-1906). Woman suffrage leader Susan B. Anthony was raised in a Quaker family in rural New York. She began teaching in local schools at an early age and from 1839 to 1849 taught at female seminaries, returning home later to run the family farm. Her parents were active participants in a variety of reform movements, and attended the first woman's rights convention, in Seneca Falls, N.Y., in 1848. Through her parents she learned of Elizabeth Cady Stanton, whom she met in 1850; the two became lifelong friends and co-workers guiding the emerging woman's rights and woman suffrage movements, with Anthony performing much of the behind-the-scenes organizing and speech-writing, and Stanton collaborating on the writing and doing much of the oratory. Together they founded the National Woman Suffrage Association and its newspaper, *The Revolution*, in 1869. For thirty years thereafter Anthony campaigned for woman suffrage at both the state and federal level, retiring at the age of 80 in 1900.

Bernstein, Eduard (1850-1932). German socialist and author, best known for his advocacy of an evolutionary rather than revolutionary path to socialism. Bernstein lived in Zurich the same time as Florence Kelley, editing a socialist periodical. He moved to London in 1888 and was influenced by Fabianism. After the repeal of anti-socialist legislation in Germany, he returned there and served as a member of the Reichstag from 1902 to 1906.

Bismarck, Otto von (1815-1898). Founder and first chancellor of the German Empire, Bismarck had studied law before he became prime minister in 1862. Until his resignation in 1890 he devoted himself to the task of uniting Germany under Prussian leadership. In the 1880s, to defeat the Social Democrats, he became the first European statesman to design a comprehensive scheme of social security, insuring people against accident, sickness and old age. Because of his extreme authoritarianism, he was known as the "iron chancellor."

Bright, John (1811-1899). See Cobden, Richard.

Butler, Josephine (1828-1906). A social reformer who focused her efforts on the protection and rehabilitation of prostitutes, Josephine Butler became Honorary Secretary of the Ladies' National Association for the Repeal of the Contagious Diseases Act of 1869, and the leading spirit in the Association's campaign to reverse legislation that its members believed gave legal sanction to prostitution by bringing the health of "fallen women" under police supervision, and threatening all women with police molestation.

Carey, Henry C. (1793-1879). Economist and publisher, Philadelphia-born Carey became in 1817 head of the leading publishing firm of Carey, Lea & Carey. In 1835 he began to write on political economy, believing that a progressive diffusion of wealth, from the richest to the poorest classes, was taking place. His writings celebrated tariffs to protect young American industries. After 1860 his tariff policies were embodied in federal law.

Catt, Carrie Chapman (1859-1947). Suffragist and peace leader, Carrie Chapman Catt grew up in frontier Wisconsin and graduated from Iowa State College in 1880. Beginning a career as a public lecturer, she developed an interest in the suffrage movement in 1887. Three years later she married George Catt who provided economic support for her reform work. She rose rapidly in the suffrage movement's leadership ranks, serving as a substitute for the aging Susan B. Anthony who in 1900 chose Catt as her successor to the presidency of the National American Woman Suffrage Association. Although she retired from the office in 1904 to care for her ill husband, her organizing genius was felt throughout the suffrage movement thereafter, and in 1915 she resumed the presidency. Between 1916 and 1920, when the Nineteenth Amendment established woman suffrage at the national level, Catt's political skills led the movement to victory.

Cobden, Richard (1804-1865) & **Bright, John** (1811-1899). Leading British liberals who began to work together in the Anti-Corn League, devoted to the repeal of government supports for wheat prices, Cobden and Bright tried to defend the rights of working people through laissez-faire economic policies. Both were influential members of Parliament, Cobden between 1841 and 1847, Bright from 1843 to 1867. The latter championed Parliamentary reform through the extension of franchise rights, and as a Quaker, stood for religious toleration.

Comstock, Ada Louise (1876-1973). The first full-time president of Radcliffe College, Ada Comstock was raised in Minnesota and attended the University of Minnesota from 1892 to 1894; she graduated from Smith College in 1897. Two years later she earned a master's degree in English, history and education at Columbia University. Hired as a assistant professor of rhetoric and oratory at the University of Minnesota in 1900, she became the first dean at Smith College, where she later served as president (1917-1918). From 1921 to 1923 she served as the first president of the American Association of University Women. As the president of Radcliffe from 1923 to 1943, she established the college as an integral part of Harvard University.

Cornell, Ezra (1807-1874). Capitalist and founder of Cornell University, Cornell was a chief figure in the development of telegraph lines in the Eastern United States. He sat in the New York State Legislature form 1861 to 1867, and cooperated with Andrew D. White in drafting and implementing legislation to found Cornell. The University reflected his democratic and practical ideas in its freedom from religious ties, its provision for the education of women, its emphasis on training in agriculture and engineering and its faculties for poor students.

Engels, Friedrich (1820-1895). Socialist theorist and author, Engels was the closest friend, collaborator and patron of Karl Marx. Born in Barmen, in the Rhineland, he participated in the Revolution of 1848, and after its failure migrated to England. There until 1869 he ran his father's cotton-spinning factory in Manchester, thereafter living in London. His writings include *The Condition of the Working Class in England in 1844* (written in 1845, translated into English by Florence Kelley in 1887). In 1886 Kelley visited Engels in London on her return to New York after her student years in Switzerland.

Furness, Henry William (1802-1896). Born in Boston, Furness became minister of the Unitarian Church in Philadelphia in 1825 after graduating from Harvard. His congregation grew rapidly under his leadership, which emphasized anti-slavery and the humanity of Jesus. He was a close friend of Ralph Waldo Emerson and of William D. Kelley.

Jacobi, Mary Putnam (1842-1906). Physician and advocate of women's rights within the medical profession, Mary Jacobi was the daughter of the founder of the publishing firm, G. P. Putnam's Sons. She graduated from the New York College of Pharmacy in 1863, and received her M.D. the following year from the Female Medical College of Pennsylvania. She worked briefly at the New England Hospital for Women and Children in Boston, and from 1866 to 1871 studied in France, where she became the first woman to enroll in the Ecole de Medecine. Returning to New York in 1872, she organized the Association for the Advancement of the Medical Education of Women, and served as its president until 1903. From 1873 to 1889 she was professor of medecine at the Women's Medical College of the New York Infirmary for Women and Children. Author of more than a hundred scholarly papers, she was best known for her 1876 essay, "The Question of Rest for Women During Menstruation," which was awarded Harvard's Boyston Prize that year. In 1873 she married Dr. Abraham Jacobi, a leading pediatrician who shared her interest in reform causes, especially the prevention of environmentally-induced disease. With Florence Kelley she helped establish the Working Women's Society of New York in the late 1880s.

Kelley, William Darrah (1814-1890). Born in Philadelphia, Florence Kelley's father left school and began to work at age eleven. His father had died when William was two years old, leaving his widowed mother with four children, William the youngest. After completing an apprenticeship as a jeweler's assistant in 1834, he began his political career by organizing working men to oppose the United States Bank—an activity that made it difficult for him to find employment in Philadelphia. For five years he lived in Boston, working as an enameller and gaining a reputation as an able political writer and speaker. Returning to Philadelphia in 1839 as a student of law, he was admitted to the bar in 1841. He rose rapidly to political eminence: In 1846 he was appointed judge in the Court of Common Pleas, and in 1860 was elected as a Republican to the first of fifteen consecutive terms representing Pennsylvania's Fourth Congressional District in the U.S. House of Representatives.

An active abolitionist, Kelley helped support Mrs. John Brown after John Brown's raid on Harper's Ferry in 1859. As a Radical Republican in the 1860s, he supported policies of racial equality in the South. After the Civil War his support of protectionist tariffs earned him the nickname "Pig-Iron" Kelley, and his longevity in the House led to the title "Father of the House." Fiery and humanitarian, he was considered the best orator among the Republicans of the House; his *Speeches, Ad-*

dresses and Letters on Industrial and Financial Questions was published in 1872. He traveled widely in the United States and Europe, and was the author of numerous other publications, including *Lincoln and Stanton* (1885) and *The Old South and the New* (1888).

Lathrop, Julia C. (1858-1932). Social settlement leader, social worker and reformer, Julia Lathrop was raised in a politically active Illinois family. Her father, an attorney, served in the state legislature as well as the U.S. Congress, and helped Lincoln establish the Republican Party in Illinois; her mother was an active suffragist.

Lathrop attended Rockford Seminary, where she met Jane Addams, and graduated from Vassar College in 1880. For a decade she assisted her father in his law office. Then, in 1890, she joined Jane Addams at Hull House, where she remained for twenty years. In 1912 she was appointed the first head of the federal Children's Bureau, created that year by Congress at the urging of Jane Addams, Florence Kelley, Lillian Wald and Lathrop herself. Until 1920 she directed studies of infant mortality, maternal mortality, child labor, juvenile courts, mothers' pensions and a multitude of other issues affecting the welfare of children. In 1918-19 she served as president of the National Conference of Social Work.

Lloyd, Henry Demarest (1847-1903). Descended from pioneering dissenters on both sides of his family, Lloyd graduated from Columbia University in 1869 and engaged in reform activity in New York until 1872, when he settled in Chicago, accepted a position with the Chicago Tribune, and married Jessie Bross, daughter of the former lieutenant-governor of Illinois. In 1881 he became the first of the "muckrakers" of the Progressive Era with his "Story of a Great Monopoly," an expose of the railroads and Standard Oil, in the *Atlantic Monthly*. For the rest of his life Lloyd devoted his considerable skills as social and economic analyst to campaigning against the dangers of rising monopolies on behalf of the independent competitor, the consumer and the worker.

In 1885 he left the *Tribune* and became a full-time reformer. His first book, *A Strike of Millionaires Against Miners* (1890), depicted industrial injustice oppressing coal-miners. His greatest work was *Wealth Against Commonwealth* (1894), an indictment of monopolies in general and Standard Oil in particular. Just before his death in 1903, while engaged in struggles on behalf of striking anthracite miners and the municipal ownership of Chicago street railways, he joined the Socialist Party.

Mill, John Stuart (1806-1873). British philosopher and economist, Mill was elected to Parliament in 1865 and took an active part in the debates on the Reform bills of 1866-67, arguing in favor of the reform of land tenure in Ireland, the reform of London government, and the representation of women. In 1869 he published *The Subjection of Women*, a classic statement of the case for woman suffrage, which was strongly shaped if not written by his wife, Harriet Taylor.

Morrill Act. Passed by Congress in 1862, this act provided land-grants to state colleges that had as their chief purpose the teaching of subjects related to agricultural and "mechanical arts" as well as science and traditional classical studies. It was named for its author, Vermont Congressman (later Senator) Justin Smith Morrill (1810-1898).

Mosher, Eliza Maria (1846-1928). Physician and educator, Eliza Mosher was born in Cayuga County, New York to Quaker parents. She began studying medecine in 1869 at the New England Hospital for Women and Children, and completed her M.D. at the University of Michigan in 1875. After serving as resident physician at the new Massachusetts Reformatory Prison for Women from 1878 to 1883, she established a private practice with Dr. Lucy Mabel Hall, a fellow graduate of the University of Michigan and former colleague at the Reformatory. From 1896 to 1902 she served as the first woman faculty member at the University of Michigan, later becoming dean of women, professor of hygiene, resident physician and director of physical education. After a bout with cancer she returned to private practice in New York, where she pioneered in the development of health services at educational institutions. For over twenty years (1905-1928) she was senior editor of the *Medical Women's Journal*.

Mott, Lucretia Coffin (1793-1889). Quaker minister and guiding light for both the antislavery and women's rights movements after 1830, Lucretia Mott began to teach school at age of fifteen. Moving to Philadelphia in 1809, two years later she married James Mott, a fellow teacher, and between 1812 and 1828 she bore six children. She was officially recognized as a minister in 1821. Around 1825 she and her husband joined the free produce movement. An early convert to Garrisonian abolitionism, Lucretia Mott helped found the Philadelphia Female Anti-Slavery Society in 1833, and in 1840 was selected to represent the Philadelphia Anti-Slavery Society at the World Anti-Slavery Congress in London. The refusal of the Congress to seat her and other female delegates was an important factor in Mott's rise to leadership in the women's rights movement. With her sister, Martha Coffin Wright, and Elizabeth Cady Stanton, Mott organized the first women's rights conference at Seneca Falls, New York, in 1848, and gave the conference's opening and closing addresses. Thereafter she devoted much of her time to campaigning for women's rights, and was named president of the Equal Rights Association in 1866. Much of her activism in the last twenty years of her life was made possible by the sustaining friendship of Sarah Pugh, who traveled with her and generally encouraged her reform ambitions.

National Consumers' League. Founded in 1899 by Josephine Shaw Lowell and other prominent women in New York City, the National Consumers' League arose from their belief that consumers could influence the conditions under which goods were produced. Under Florence Kelley's leadership from its founding until her death in 1932, the League became after 1900 the single most important lobbying group for the passage of labor and social welfare legislation at the state and federal levels. Orchestrating the activities of some sixty-four local leagues by 1910, the NCL maintained a federal system with a national board setting policies that were frequently adopted by the local boards. As the General Secretary Florence Kelley oversaw an association that included elite, middle-class and working-class members. Its membership was primarily, though not entirely, female, and its presidents were often leading Progressives, such as Richard Ely and Newton Baker.

Pugh, Sarah (1800-1884). Teacher and leader in the anti-slavery and women's rights movement, Sarah Pugh was born into a Quaker family. Since her father died when she was three years old, Sarah was raised solely by her mother, who worked in Philadelphia as a dressmaker. She began teaching in 1821 and in 1829 established her own school, where she taught for more than a decade. She became a Garrisonian abolitionist in 1835, and joined the Philadelphia Female Anti-Slavery Society, serving for more than thirty years as its presiding officer. The Anti-Slavery Convention of American Women met in Pugh's schoolrooms in 1838, when a mob burned down Pennsylvania Hall, where they had been meeting. She was a leader in the movement to petition Congress to abolish slavery, and the Pennsylvania Anti-Slavery Society often met in her home. In 1840 she accompanied Lucretia Mott and other women delegates to the World Anti-Slavery Congress, and wrote a stirring protest when women were excluded from the convention. After the Civil War she served as Lucretia Mott's traveling companion, making it possible for Mott to continue her leadership of the women's rights movement in her 70's and 80's.

Rankin, Jeannette (1880-1973). Born in Montana Territory, and a graduate of the University of Montana in 1902, Rankin was the first woman elected to the U.S. House of Representatives (1915), and the only member of Congess to oppose U.S. entry into both world wars. In 1919 she accompanied Jane Addams and Florence Kelley to Zurich to the Second International Congress of Women, which founded the Women's International League for Peace and Freedom. In 1920 Kelley appointed Rankin field secretary of the National Consumers' League, and until 1924 she lobbied for social legislation such as the Sheppard-Towner Maternity and Infancy Protection Act, which sought to diminish the high U.S. infant and maternal mortality rates. She also led educational campaigns in the Mississippi Valley in favor of laws to regulate working conditions for Women. From 1929 to 1939 she worked as a Washington lobbyist for the National Council for the Prevention of War. In 1940 she was re-elected to Congress, and cast the sole vote against American entry into World War II, making her re-election in 1942 impossible. Throughout the 1950s she opposed the Cold War and in the next decade, she demonstrated against the war in Vietnam.

Shaw, Anna Howard (1847-1919). Minister, lecturer, and suffragist, Anna Howard Shaw assumed much of the responsibility for her family's support at the age of twelve, when her father and older brothers left their frontier claim in Michigan and her mother suffered a mental breakdown. She began to teach at the age of fifteen, and nine years later was licensed as a Methodist preacher. In 1878 she graduated from the divinity school of Boston University, and in 1880 was ordained as the first woman minister in the Methodist Protestant Church, serving as pastor to two churches, Methodist and Congregational, on Cape Cod. Seeking greater challenges in her life, she began to study medicine in 1885 at Boston University, where she received her M.D. in 1886. Her life-long work in the suffrage campaign began in 1885, when she became a lecturer and organizer for the Massachusetts Women Suffrage Association. She entered the national suffrage movement by leading the Franchise Department of the Woman's Christian Temperance Union from 1888 to 1892. That year she became vice-president of the National American Woman Suffrage Association, holding this position until 1904, when she became president, acting in that capacity until 1916.

Sheppard-Towner Maternity and Infant Protection Act (1921-1927). Passed due to intensive lobbying by a large coalition of women's organizations led by Florence Kelley just after the adoption of the Nineteenth Amendment provided for woman suffrage, the Act was designed to reduce the extraordinarily high infant and maternal mortality rates in the United Sates. It authorized an appropriation of approximately seven and a half million dollars in federal funds allocated to states through the U. S. Children's Bureau; the amount each state received depended on its population and matching funds it provided. As historian J. Stanley Lemons noted in a chapter on the Act in *The Woman Citizen: Social Feminism in the 1920s* (University of Illinois Press, 1973), "The law provided for instruction in the hygiene of maternity and infancy through public health nurses, visiting nurses, consultation centers, child-care conferences, and literature distribution."(p.159)

In 1923 the U.S. Supreme Court approved the constitutionality of the Act, but its opponents, including the American Medical Association and right-wing political organizations such as the Woman Patriots and the Sentinels of the Republic, relentlessly attacked it as a conspiracy to "Sovietize" the United States. In 1927 Congress allowed the act to die by not renewing its funding. Nevertheless the program had proved so valuable that sixteen states appropriated sufficient funds to match or exceed previous expenditures, and twenty-nine others continued some form of funding. In the Social Security Act of 1935 the federal government resumed appropriations for maternal and infancy protection and for dependent children.

Starr, Ellen Gates (1859-1940). Settlement leader and co-founder with Jane Addams of Hull House in 1889, Ellen Gates Starr was raised in Illinois and studied at Rockford Seminary in 1877-78, where she met Jane Addams. After teaching in Chicago for ten years and traveling in Europe with Addams, the two friends started a settlement that immediately won the support of the city's wealthy patrons of reform. Especially interested in bringing the power of the western tradition of fine arts and literature to the urban poor, Starr founded and became the first president of the Chicago Public School Art Society. One of the most politically radical members of Hull House, she joined Florence Kelley in her battle against sweatshop working conditions, and in 1896, 1910 and 1915 played a central part in supporting striking garment workers. In 1903 she was a founding member of the Illinois branch of the National Women's Trade Union League.

Stevens, Alzina Parsons (1849-1900). Labor leader, journalist and settlement worker, Alzina Stevens was born and raised in Maine. After the death of her father, she went to work in a textile factory at the age of thirteen, and lost her right index finger in an industrial injury. Divorced soon after an early marriage, she retained her husband's name. By the time she was eighteen she had learned the printing trade; she settled in Chicago, joined Typographical Union No.16, and in 1877 organized Working Woman's Union Number 1. Between 1882 and 1891 she worked in Toledo for the *Toledo Bee* and became chief officer of twenty-two local assemblies of the Knights of Labor after organizing a woman's assembly. At the national convention of the People's Party in 1892 she represented the labor organizations of northwestern Ohio. Returning to Chicago that year, she became a resident of Hull House. The following year she was appointed Assistant Factory Inspector of the State of Illinois—Florence Kelley was Chief Factory Inspector. The two women led the victorious enforcement of pioneering labor legislation for women and children, and compiled valuable social statistics, published in 1895 in *Hull House Maps and Papers*. After she and Kelley were replaced by a new governor, Stevens in 1899 became the first probation officer of the newly established Cook County Juvenile Court Committee, supervising a staff of six.

Lady Stanley of Alderley (1807-1895). Promoter of British women's education, including a medical college for women, and a moving spirit of the Women's Liberal Unionist Association.

Duchess of Sutherland (Harriet Elizabeth Georgiana Leveson-Gower, 1806-1868). A philanthropist who organized upper- and middle-class British women against American slavery in the 1850s, the Duchess of Sutherland served between 1837 and 1841 as the mistress of the robes to Queen Victoria.

Thomas, Martha Carey (1857-1935). Educator and feminist, M. Carey Thomas was born to a wealthy Quaker family in Baltimore. Graduating from Cornell in 1877, she studied literature at the University of Zurich, where she was the first woman to receive a PhD in 1882. Appointed professor/of English at the newly founded Quaker college for women, Bryn Mawr, where her father and other relatives were trustees, she became president in 1894, and held that position until 1922. In 1908 she became the first president of the National College Women's Equal Suffrage League.

United States Children's Bureau (1912-1962). Founded in 1912 after an eight-year campaign led by Florence Kelley, Lillian Wald and Julia Lathrop, the Children's Bureau was lodged in the U.S. Bureau of Labor. Until 1920 it was headed by Julia Lathrop, and during the 1920s by Grace Abbot. Its first efforts were devoted to documenting and reducing high infant and maternal mortality rates among the urban and rural poor. These efforts formed the basis for the passage of the Sheppard-Towner Act. Soon after its founding the Bureau focused on the harmful effects of child labor. Perhaps the best example of the political power of middle-class women reformers in the Progressive Era, the Bureau was run by them despite the opposition of state public health officials who viewed them as amateur troublemakers.

Wright, Carroll D. (1840-1909). Social statistician, economist and public official, Wright studied law and fought in the Civil War as a youth, settling thereafter in Boston, where he worked as a patent lawyer and served two terms in the state legislature. In 1873 he was appointed chief of the Massachusetts Bureau of Statistics of Labor by the Governor, the first such bureau in the U.S. In 1885 Wright became the first Commissioner of the U.S. Bureau of Labor. His paramount influence on the development of labor statistics in the U.S. during the last decades of the nineteenth century and the first years of the twentieth is shown by his organization in 1883 of the National Convention of Chiefs and Commissioners of Bureaus of Statistics of Labor (of which he was president for almost twenty years), his role as chairman of the federal commission that investigated the Pullman Strike of 1894, his position as recorder of the commission that investigated the coal strike of 1902, and his activities as president of the American Statistical Association from 1897 until his death.

For a hundred years,
the Charles H. Kerr Company
has published pro-labor & socialist literature.
That's what we were doing back in the days
of the Pullman Strike—and that's what
we're still doing today.

Send for our complete catalog.

CHARLES H. KERR PUBLISHING COMPANY
1740 West Greenleaf Avenue, Suite 7
Chicago, Illinois 60626

Other Books From Charles H. Kerr

HAYMARKET SCRAPBOOK
Edited by Dave Roediger & Franklin Rosemont

Profusely illustrated oversize compilation on the most world-reverberating event in American labor history: the Haymarket Affair of 1886. Original articles by William J. Adelman, Carlotta Anderson, Carolyn Ashbaugh, Paul Avrich, Alan Dawley, Richard Drinnon, Philip Foner, Fred Thompson & many others, as well as numerous reprints of articles, reminiscences, poems & tributes by Kate Austin, Voltairine de Cleyre, Clarence Darrow, Eugene Debs, Elizabeth Gurley Flynn, Emma Goldman, Bill Haywood, Lizzie Holmes, Mother Jones, Lucy Parsons, Carl Sandburg *et al.*, plus translations from the Chinese, Italian, Yiddish, etc., & scarce texts by the Chicago Martyrs themselves. $11.95

THE AUTOBIOGRAPHY OF MOTHER JONES

First published by Kerr in 1925, the new edition of this exciting memoir of the "Miners' Angel" includes the original foreword by Clarence Darrow and a new biographical introduction by IWW historian Fred Thompson. $6.95

LUCY PARSONS: AMERICAN REVOLUTIONARY
by Carolyn Ashbaugh

The first full-length biography of an outstanding figure in American labor history. A noted agitator in Haymarket days and later a founding member of the IWW, Lucy Parsons inspired three generations of labor activists. The police regarded this black workingclass woman as "more dangerous than a thousand rioters." $6.95

REASONS FOR PARDONING THE HAYMARKET ANARCHISTS
by John Peter Altgeld

Gov. Altgeld's classic pardon message has long been out of print. This new Kerr/Haymarket Centennial edition includes a tribute to Altgeld by Clarence Darrow and a new introduction by Leon M. Despres. "The calmest, clearest, most incisive and most factual dissertation on that stirring case" (Harry Barnard, *Eagle Forgotten*). $3.95

WRITE FOR OUR COMPLETE CATALOG

Charles H. Kerr Publishing Company
Established 1886
1740 West Greenleaf Avenue, Suite 7
Chicago, Illinois 60626